PROJECTS / PROCESSES VOLUME III

Continued Traditions & Histories of Performing Arts

PROJECTS / PROCESSES VOLUME III

Continued Traditions & Histories of Performing Arts

Series Editor: Senjuti Mukherjee

HARPER DESIGN
An Imprint of HarperCollins*Publishers*

First published in India in 2019 by
HarperCollins *Publishers*
A-75, Sector 57, Noida, Uttar Pradesh 201301, India
www.harpercollins.co.in

2 4 6 8 10 9 7 5 3 1

P-ISBN: 978-93-5357-532-8

Typeset in 9/14.2 Freight at
Serendipity Arts Foundation

Printed and bound at
Replika Press Pvt. Ltd.

Contents

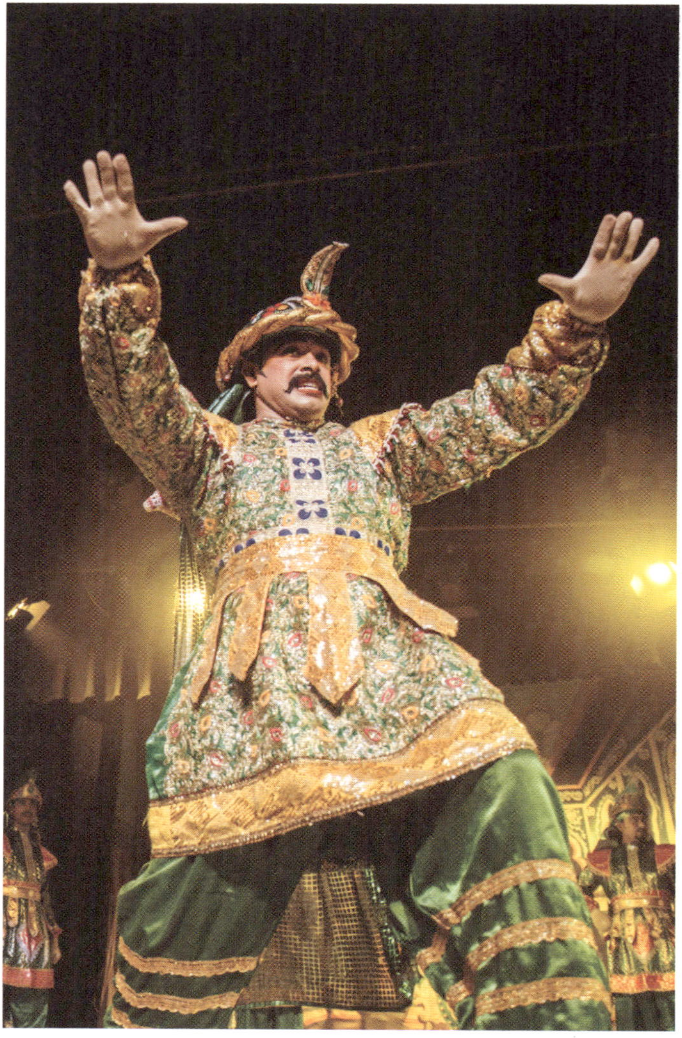

All images from the performance as well as behind the scenes of *Karalsman*, performed at the Large Open Air Theatre, Kala Academy at Serendipity Arts Festival, 2018.

Karalsman

Curated by Leela Samson

Venue Large Open Air Theatre, Kala Academy

Karalsman

Collaborator *Yuvajana Chavittu Nataka Kala Samithy Director Thampi Payyapilly (Ashan)*
Written by *Chinna Thampi Annavi Avatharanam Yuvajana Chavittunadaka Kala Samithy*
Curator *Leela Samson*

Chavittu Natakam originated in the coastal belt of western Kerala during the sixteenth and seventeenth century, together with the advent of the Christian Missionaries. Closely connected to Koothu and Koodiyattam of Kerala, the dance form also bears striking resemblance to the Greek Opera. While in the olden days, the performance of a single story of Chavittu Natakam extended between ten to fifteen days, it has now been confined to a short span of two hours. The story of this play is based on the heroic deeds of the French emperor Karalsman (Charlemagne), who defeated Albrath, the emperor of Jerusalem, regaining the land he had once lost.

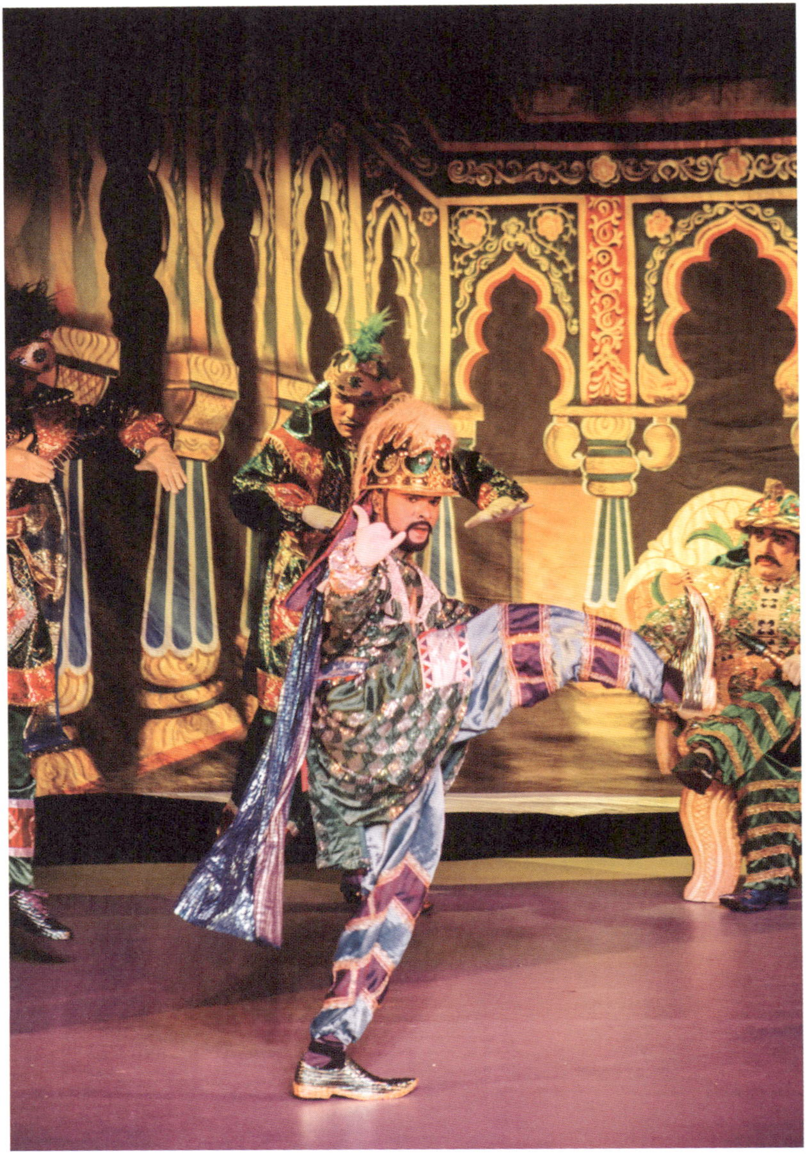

Kings of Shoreline: A Performance of *Karalsman* Chavittu Nadakam

AKHILA VIMAL C.

As the stage lights up, we see the court of Karalsman (Charlemagne), former king of the Franks, positioned on a throne at the centre, flanked on each side by three performers in vibrant, glittering costumes reminiscent of medieval Roman soldiers. While the king sits cross-legged, his soldiers move vigorously, stamping their feet and jumping in rhythm with an adulatory song about their ruler. The dance sequence begins with pounding steps, one foot after the other, while slightly winding the upper body. Standing in a slanted position, the six performers turn around, bringing their hands to their mouth and showing the gesture they state, "hereby, I say." They repeat the gestures as they approach the audience, swaying and stamping with force, pointing fingers at the audience as the tempo of the song transforms. The performers fold and fling their arms as the song is followed by a two-fold onset of *Vaythari*, or oral commands, and *Kalasam*, which marks the end of the sequential movement. The Kalasam consists of various steps—the movements are rhythmic and symmetrical—and in the end, performers return to their original position and stand with their hands on their waists, looking first at the king and then the audience with valour.

Karalsman then gets up from the throne and walks downstage while the other performers dance behind him. He is wearing a glittering outfit: a red circlet crown embellished with golden metal, surmounted by ornaments and a cross on the top, while holding a sceptre.

The above describes a performance of *Karalsman Chavittu Nadakam* by the Kerala theatre group Yuvajana Chavittunadaka Kalasamithy at Panjim's Kala Academy, as part of Serendipity Art Festival 2018. Written by Chinnathambi Annavi, *Karalsman Charitham* (translated as the "story of Karalsman") is considered the first and most popular play among performers of Chavittu Nadakam, a Latin Christian art form originating in Kerala's Ernakulam district. Annavi, believed to be a Tamilian, came to Kerala in the sixteenth century and became deeply influenced by Christianity, writing numerous plays before returning to Tamil Nadu. However, Sabeena Rafi, one of the revivalists of Chavittu Nadakam, argues that he might have been a foreign missionary who came to India, learned the language and picked an Indian name to spread Christianity. Often addressed as the father of Chavittu Nadakam, Annavi has written the majority of the genre's plays, and is its most celebrated author.

As a Christian art form, Chavittu Nadakam originated from Kerala's links to the Portuguese. "Chavittu" means foot pounding and "nadakam" refers to theatre, so it is not surprising that this musical drama centres around its emphasis on foot movement. Chavittu Nadakam is believed to have been harnessed by Christian missionaries during the sixteenth century to spread religion. Though the local origin is manifest in the use of coastal Tamil in both musical style and the lyrics , the performance form draws significantly from European costumes and operatic presentation. European opera typically comprises of musical narratives, shimmering costumes and a stage without curtains, all of which seem to make their way into Chavittu Nadakam, which can be seen as a cultural tool that the Portuguese used in Kerala to entertain and educate people about Christianity, as the narratives celebrate those who advocated the religion. The natives of Gothuruth, a small island in central Kerala, are still preserving the form, though it has lost its theological intent. Sabeena Rafi, in her book *Chavittu Nadakam* (1980) argues that, Christianity existed in India even prior to the advent of Europeans but Christians[1] were more interested in indigenous beliefs. They were also part of Hindu religious celebrations and temple rituals even after conversion. Christians in Kerala popularly believe that they were converted from upper-caste *namboothiris*. The converted *namboothiris* were not ready to leave their cultural traditions and advocated organising *Kuthu* and *Kutiyattam* performances in the churches. *Udayamperoor Sunnahadose*[2] (The Synod of Diamper), however, restricted Kutiyattam and Kuthu along with other rituals from the church space. This led to a cultural vacuum among native communities which forced them to create an art form to fill the void left by the demolition of traditional forms.[3]

The evolution of Chavittu Nadakam, and the European influence on its performance and costumes can thus be seen as the result of Udayamperoor Sunnahadose's establishment of rules and regulations. Sabeena Rafi's argument about the cultural void left behind by Kuthu and Kutiyattam seems problematic, as these forms were already in the hands of Brahmin priests from thirteenth century onwards, and were only performed in Kuthambalams, or theatres located on temple premises.[4] Through the readings of Sunnahadose, one could come to the assumption that the coastal Christians (Latin Catholic in the context of Kerala) adapted the revival of churches from native belief system and Roman superiority prior to other groups who believe that they converted from Hindu upper castes (Thaliath, 1958).[5] Chavittu Nadakam was born out of the cultural flexibility of the marginalised. When the laws of Sunnahadose catechised beliefs and cultural practices, these communities riposted by creating a form that interwove existing cultural cognizance and newly invented ecumenical setting. Fr. Joseph Valiyaveettil, in his book on Chavittu Nadakam points out its similarities to *Terukuthu*, an ancient Tamil performance form that draws on epic mythology. He asserts that the songs, dialogues and presentation of these two forms correspond to each other frequently,[6] an idea that seems more convincing than the existing narrative of Chavittu Nadakam replacing Kuthu and Kutiyattam. If one closely observes the cultural and historical settings of Chavittu Nadakam, it is not difficult to conclude that the art form did not borrow much from Kuthu and Kutiyattam. However, Terukuthu and its narrative tradition, constituting of music and dance, could be seen as an early form of Chavittu Nadakam.

Despite European stylisation, the pattern of music and movements are therefore influenced by a traditional Tamil form. The language used in the form further validates this argument.

Having played a vital role in the Romanisation of Christianity in Kerala, Chavittu Nadakam went on to become a form of entertainment amongst the central region's coastal community, who freed itself from the philosophical and propagandist elements. Joseph Valiyaveettil observes that the evolution of Chavittu Nadakam started from heroic stories and moved through devotional and Biblical ones to eventually adapt community stories.[7] By the beginning of twentieth century, the popularity of Chavittu Nadakam waned and the tradition stopped thriving. In the post-independence landscape of India, the tradition began drawing attention in a novel nationalist setting. The performance practices across India played their own roles in renewed cultural revival movements. Chavittu Nadakam, which had largely lost its performance space and audience, was given a new lease of life in the freshly evolved nationalist context. The form has since gained popularity in the contemporary, and has even gained stages outside Kerala. Interestingly, the most performed piece among all the Chavittu Nadakams is *Karalsman Charitham*, and there are some remarkable regional contexts that led to the popularity of *Karalsman*.

KARALSMAN CHAVITTU NADAKAM: A FOREWORD TO PERFORMATIVE REGION

Karalsman Charitham traditionally had five acts enacted by a hundred performers over fifteen days. However, the long-lasting performance is no longer in practice. The contemporary performances normally do not last more than three hours. Sajan, a performer from Yuvajana Chavittunadaka Kalasamithy, states that during his childhood, Chavittu Nadakam would typically be staged for five days as each act needed one day. "Now it is divided into four separate plays and *Karalsman Nadakam* is one of them; in the current scenario, the play is altered and gets performed in a few hours," Sajan tells me. The performance at Serendipity Arts Festival lasted for an hour, covering two acts followed by an end sequence where the troupe thanked God for helping them complete the play successfully.

Karalsman celebrates the story of its eponymous eighth-century emperor, who was known in the West as Charlemagne and also called the Father of Europe. Karalsman was the first to unite significant parts of Western Europe since the classical era of the Roman Empire. By the end of the eighth century, Karalsman was crowned the Emperor of the Romans. The heroic narratives on Charlemagne were popular in Europe till the twentieth century. *Karalsman Nadakam* in particular chronicles the battle to recapture Jersualem's holy sites between Karalsman and his enemy Al-biranth, the emperor of Turkey. The first scene shows the king asking his minister Galalon (Ganalon) about the well-being of his people. Soon after, he asks the minister to announce war against emperor of Turkey. The second scene is where Al-biranth receives this message and resolves to go to war with Karalsman; the battle and his eventual victory is showcased in the following sequence. Joly Puthussery argues that plays of Chavittu Nadakam, other than *Karalsman*, were performed in rural areas, at harvest and during the festivals of patron saints in coastal regions. However, plays like *Karalsman* and other forms which celebrate wars and heroism always had elaborative stage performances.[8]

The popularity of *Karalsman* cannot be assessed without understanding the regional context of war as a heroic subject. Kerala, as a region, celebrates war through its performance, whether it is classical forms like Kathakali or rituals like *Teyyam*. All such forms have the universal motive of war, killing and hero-worship. Sabeena Rafi writes, "the *Sunnahadose* had ended the system of wearing weapons on one's body and the presentation of martial arts during festivals, saying it will lead to wounds and even death and it propagates vengefulness. Thus, the people needed at least an artistic venture that could divert their physical strength and training. The war stories of *Karalsman* gave them an opportunity to depict their war instinct."[9] Though her argument is about the formation of Chavittu

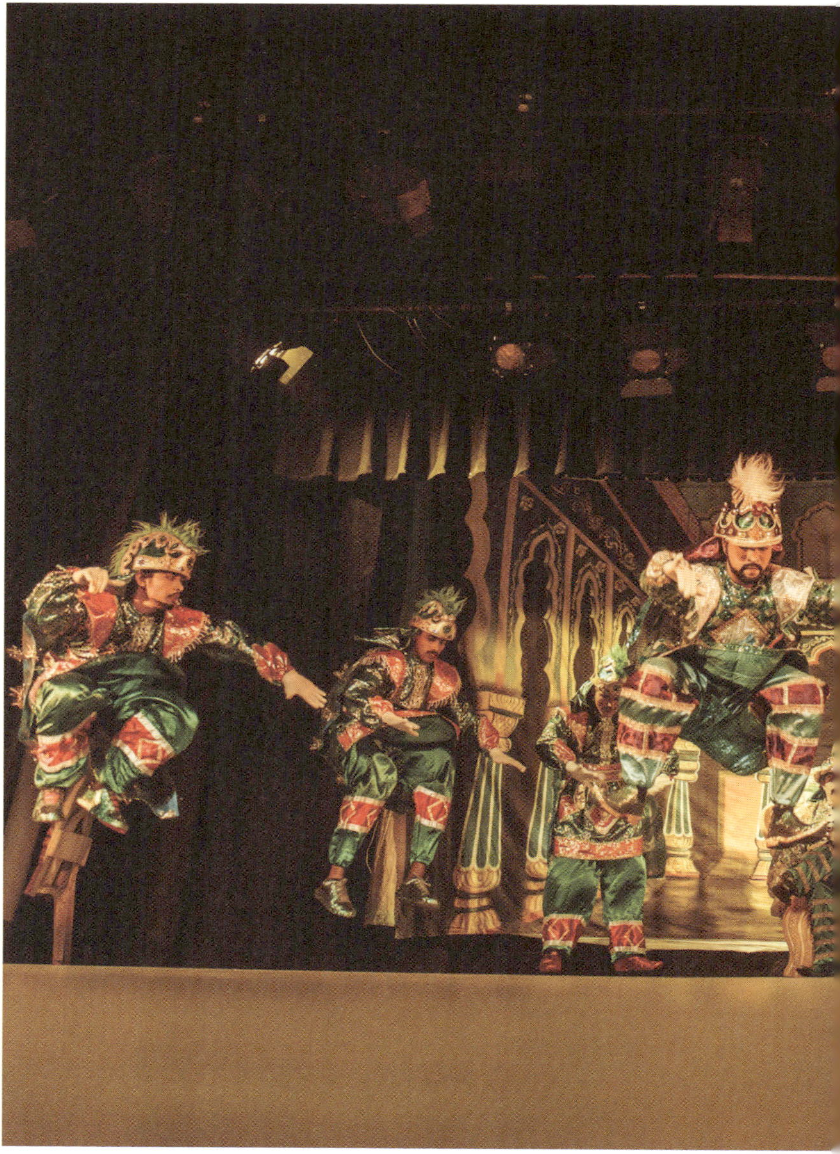

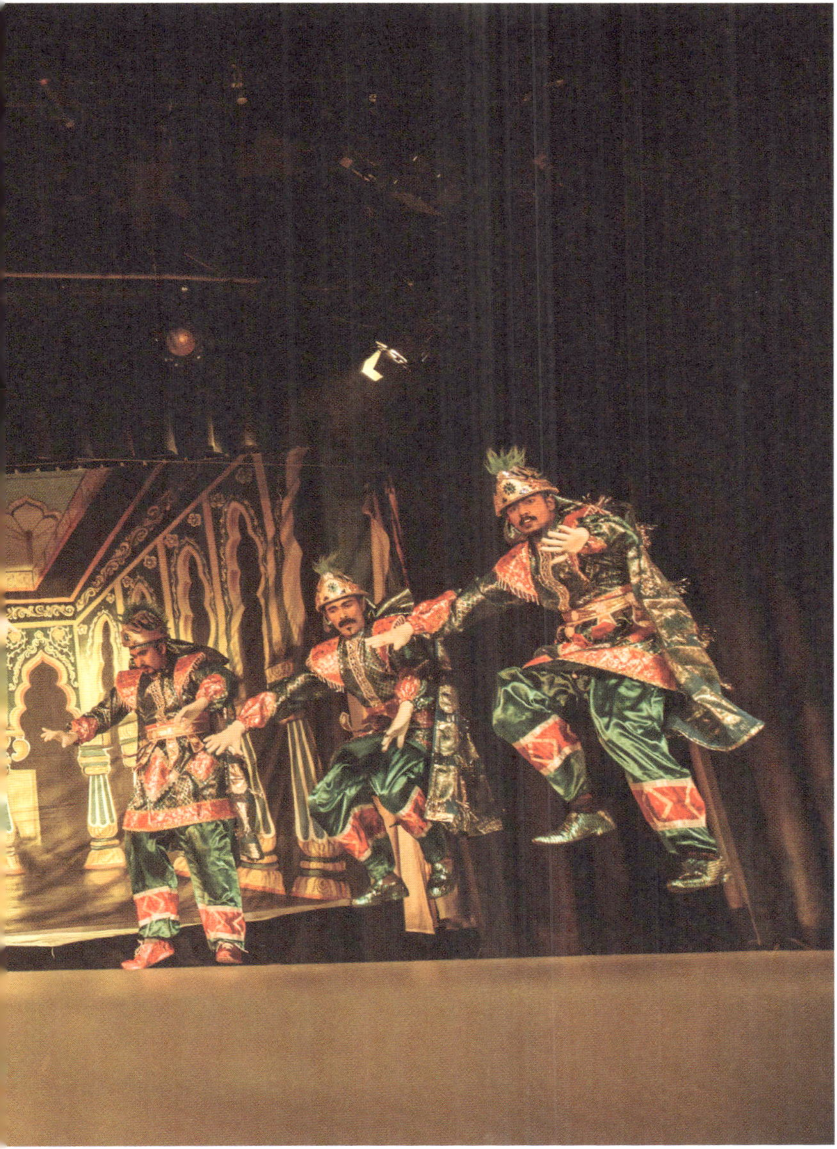

Nadakam, these points are further valid because the region and its theatrical traditions still cultivate the performance of war, among which *Karalsman's* story is one.

The choreography and motifs of performance in the play are particularly important. The foot-stamping, from which the performance derives its nomenclature, as well as the rigour and stylisation, epitomises the idea of war. The later plays are mostly allied with devotional stories which are intended to spread Christian philosophy. Devotional plays usually have a slow-paced narrative not suitable for a form like Chavittu Nadakam, which relies entirely on the rapid tempo of the performance. Another important consideration is that devotional performance has lost its originary purpose as it is no longer used for spreading faith and instead meant solely for entertainment. Therefore, the entire narrative should come to a juncture where it gets maximum output from the stylisation of the performance. According to Thambi Payyapilly Ashan, who directs the latest adaptation of *Karalsman Nadakam*, "the performance of Karalsman is much acclaimed for its rigour and war narrative and people like it more than any other play as it communicates more to the core of the form. Chavittu Nadakam, without war and battle cry, will not satisfy the audience as they come to watch a vigorous form. Other than that, *Karalsman Nadakam* is the only play written in Senthamizh—an early variant of the Tamil language—which itself gives rhythm to the performance." Ashan further states that as a performer, he enjoys acting along with Senthamizh lyrics.

The language in the region is another context one needs to understand while looking at a Chavittu Nadakam performance. While the literature uses Tamil, the majority of the performers and audience members don't actually understand the language; populations in the coastal belt of Kerala, where this performance is prevalent in practice, do not have a recent history of using Tamil. The primary forms of communication are the dynamic, expressive movements. The *Karalsman Nadakam* is evidence of the form's endurance, reaching spectators across language barriers and purely through performance.

It is also important to note that though the story of Karalsman has lost its popularity in Europe, it is still being staged in a small island in central Kerala today. In order to understand the nuances of Chavittu Nadakam as an existing form, we need to consider the region and its performativity, where region should be looked upon as a relational space, which has more performative and affective strategies than an absolute geographical boundary. It is also essential to understand whether it is the trope of war or the energy of the performance that constitute the identity of the form. Ultimately, the performance needs to be studied by seeing who watches it and for whom it is being staged, particularly in the context of Chavittu Nadakam, which cannot be analysed by detaching it from the geographical and emotional terrain it is associated with.

GOTHURUTH TO WORLD STAGE: A PERFORMANCE ANALYSIS

In a conversation with the festival's curator of dance, Leela Samson, she explained some of the reasons behind bringing this performance to Goa: "The Portuguese and coastal connection made me think that it would be nice to bring the form which the Portuguese had brought to Kerala's coast. Further, even after losing its philosophical intent, of playing a role in missionary activities, it is still getting staged in the coastal regions of Kerala. Vividly, Goa also has a history of Portuguese invention which only left architectural and food traditions, but in Kerala they left behind a tradition of performance which was nurtured by the people of coastal Kerala. I was excited at the viewership received by the performance in Goa."

Bringing one coastal form to another coastal region, which shares a history of colonisation, was a thoughtful process. Samson says that "the classical forms in India had enough exposure and this is the time we should think of giving space to other forms as they also have many things to share with us." When I watched the performance at Gothuruthu, I was in awe of how this form survived though the centuries, despite losing its original theological intentions. As someone who has watched Chavittu Nadakam at Gothuruthu, and across different stages in Kerala, I was apprehensive about its reception in a larger setting such as Serendipity. However, it was one of the most packed stages at the festival, with both Goan and outside audiences in attendance. I interviewed people belonging to both categories. For the Goan people the colourful and vigorous spectacle of Chavittu Nadakam was something that enlivens the stage. Moreover, knowing the story of Charlemagne and similarity with European opera are other factors that brought them close to the performance. On the contrary, the other set raised the issue of civility in the performance. However, the context of performance and the life of performers that got reflected on stage were things that both the set of spectators failed to relate with.

One of the main motifs lacking from the Chavittu Nadakam performance at Serendipity was the Chavittu itself, the particular quality of loud and hard foot-stamping on a wooden stage. The performance at the festival was on a concrete floor that couldn't replicate the same effect. Traditionally performed on a wooden floor called *tattu*, loud beats form an essential part of the performance, amplified by special knee-high boots made of leather with a wooden sole that is tight around the leg shaft and ankle. The construction of the contemporary portrayal is most concerned with the visual spectacle, resulting in the performers at Serendipity wearing sparkling shoes to match their costumes, and giving the traditional boots a miss. The Chavittu Nadakam stages were built to enhance these beats as well, which is achieved through wooden panels placed on empty barrels that produce loud reverberations. Though the use of barrels is rare now, the wooden stages are still in vogue. Conventionally, the performance is considered a success if the wooden panel of the stage is caved by the time the final sequence is completed, an act that gives Chavittu Nadakam its other name—*Tattu Polippan Nadakam*, or "drama that smashes the stage." In colloquial usage *Tattu Polippan* indicates an accomplishment.

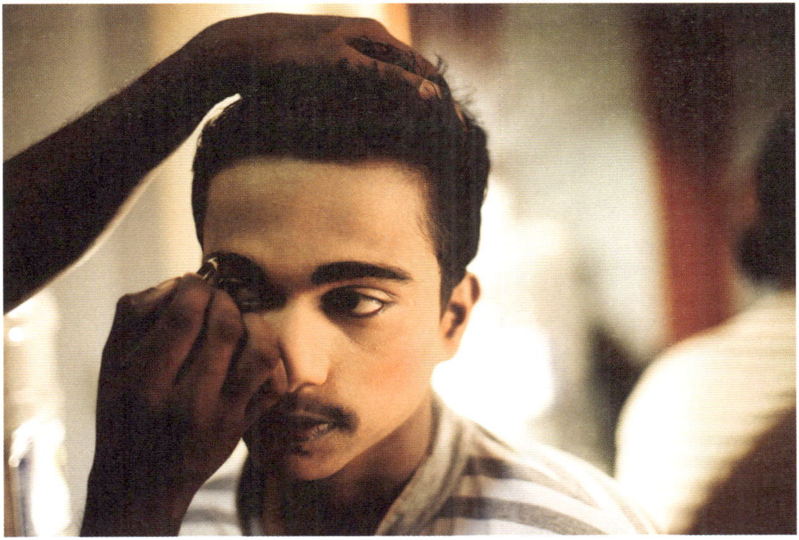

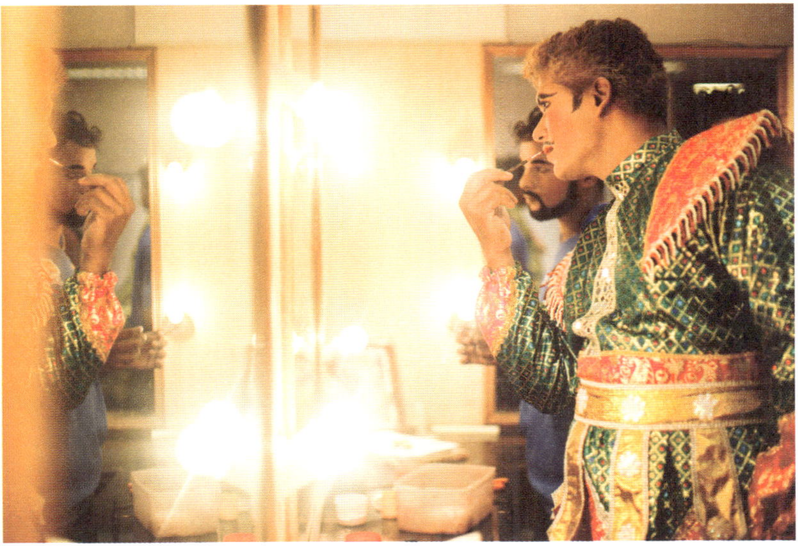

Originally hailing from the fishermen community of central Kerala, today this performance form mostly survives in Gothuruth Island. The performers are mainly from fishermen communities and other labour classes like construction workers and autorickshaw drivers. In Gothuruth, there are mainly three groups that practice and perform Chavittu Nadakam. For the people of Gothuruth, this tradition is part of their lives and most of them are associated with it. Evenings on the island are pulsating with the beats of practice sessions or presentations. The fishermen go to the sea in the mornings and in the evening, they transform into kings and soldiers. Joseph Valiyaveettil calls the genre of Chavittu Nadakam songs *Kadalora Pattukal*, or songs of the shoreline. In recent years, Gothuruth and its performance tradition has started attracting tourists to the island, giving it the name "Island of Festivals."

The cultural conflicts of living a dual life are visible among the people in the island. Thambi Payyampilly, the chief performer and teacher of Yuvajana Chavittunadaka Kalasamithy, the leading troupe of Gothuruth, primarily earns his living as an auto driver. During a conversation with Payyampilly at the festival venue in Goa, he said that, "for the people of Gothuruth, Chavittu Nadakam is an emotion that makes us live our life. We don't consider it a means of living; rather it is a lifestyle. No aspects in our lives evade the proximity of Chavittu Nadakam. Almost every evening we come together, after our prospective work to train students and practice the form. While in the costume we are the kings and soldiers, and when out of it, we are manual labourers. People who perform Chavittu Nadakam always live this dual life unlike in many other mainstream forms."

The new generation of performers are more diverse and while some of them have jobs in cities, most remain fishermen and labourers. For them, Chavittu Nadakam is both a passion and a regional identity. In Gothuruth, most children are trained in the form and some continue to pursue it in the future. But even while Gothuruthu and its people are keeping the tradition alive by passing it from generation to generation, the discussion around its revival and stylisation is also on edge.

According to Sabeena Rafi, refining the form was important as it will help to bring people out of Gothuruth. She suggested different layers of alteration in the performance in order to revive the form. Rafi proposed condensing the performance to two to three hours, the duration of a film, which the performers eventually followed. She further states that Chavittu Nadakam, being a classical form, should get more attention and proper training in the same way that Kathakali was revived following the Natyashastra.[10] Rafi, the first to intensely study the context of Chavittu Nadakam and having spent her life in Gothuruth, seems to have the most troubled idea of refinement and revival of this form. One can be curious enough to engage with the question of whether an art form can ever escape the categorisation of "classical" or "folk." As dance studies scholar Uttara Asha Coorlawala argues, "'classical' is distinguished from 'folk' by its alignment with the concept of 'samskriti' or refined action. Audience involvement is limited to aesthetic appreciation rather than ritualistic communal participation and dissolution of differences".[11] The political and power dynamics of classicisation have always existed and been a matter of scrutiny. Hence, it is important to look into the discussions of refinement and stylisation of an art form which has not been a subject of nationalisation or political perusal. However, Rafi's suggestion to refine the form by linking it with the Natyashastra has never come to the forefront. Another important factor that helped the form escape political scrutiny might be its identity as a Christian tradition, as the Natyashastra was always affiliated with the so-called Hindu art forms. It is important to note that there are several criticisms on the need of aestheticisation and professionalism in Chavittu Nadakam presentations.

American avant-garde choreographer Yvonne Rainer states that the performers "give absolutely no attention to production finesse. They miss cues, they look around 'out of character,' the curtain keeps sticking, the two light men run up from the pit where they have been operating the spotlights seemingly at random and carry a banner across the stage, then scamper back down".[12] Curator Leela Samson also felt the performance was a bit messy considering the

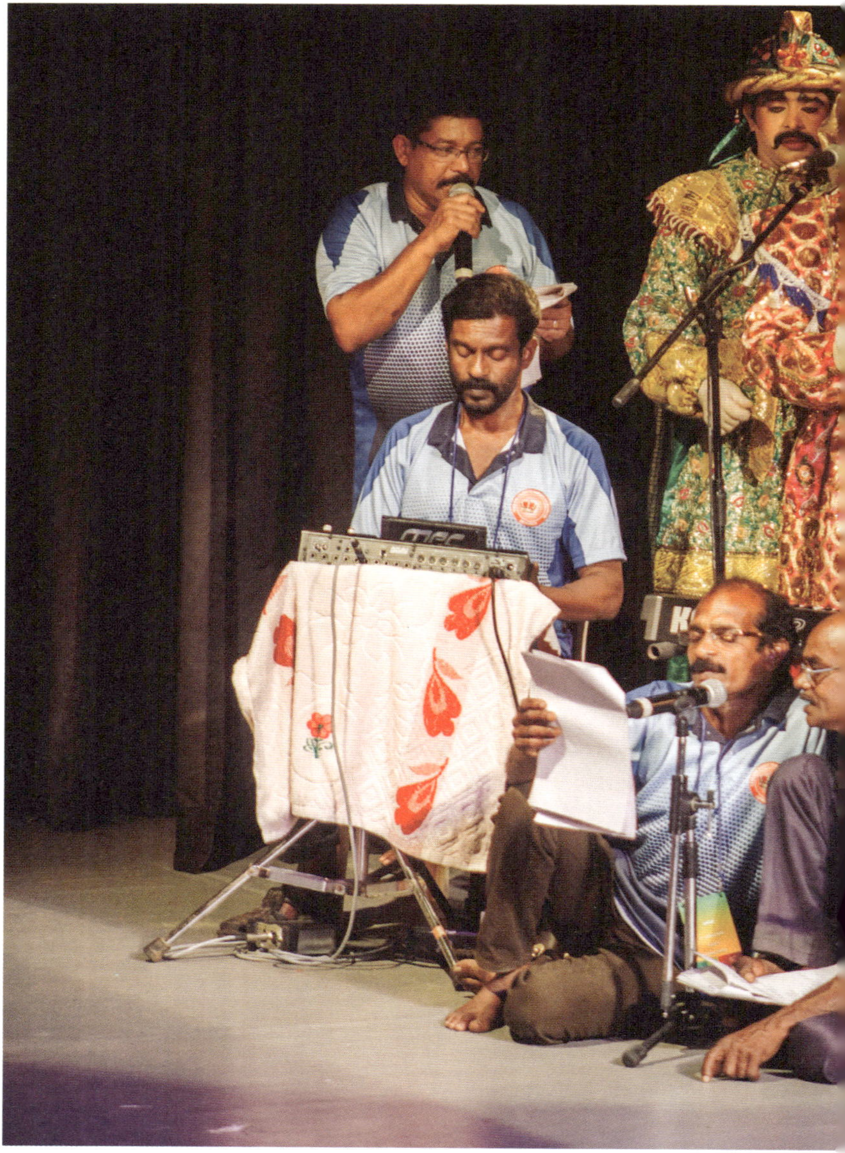

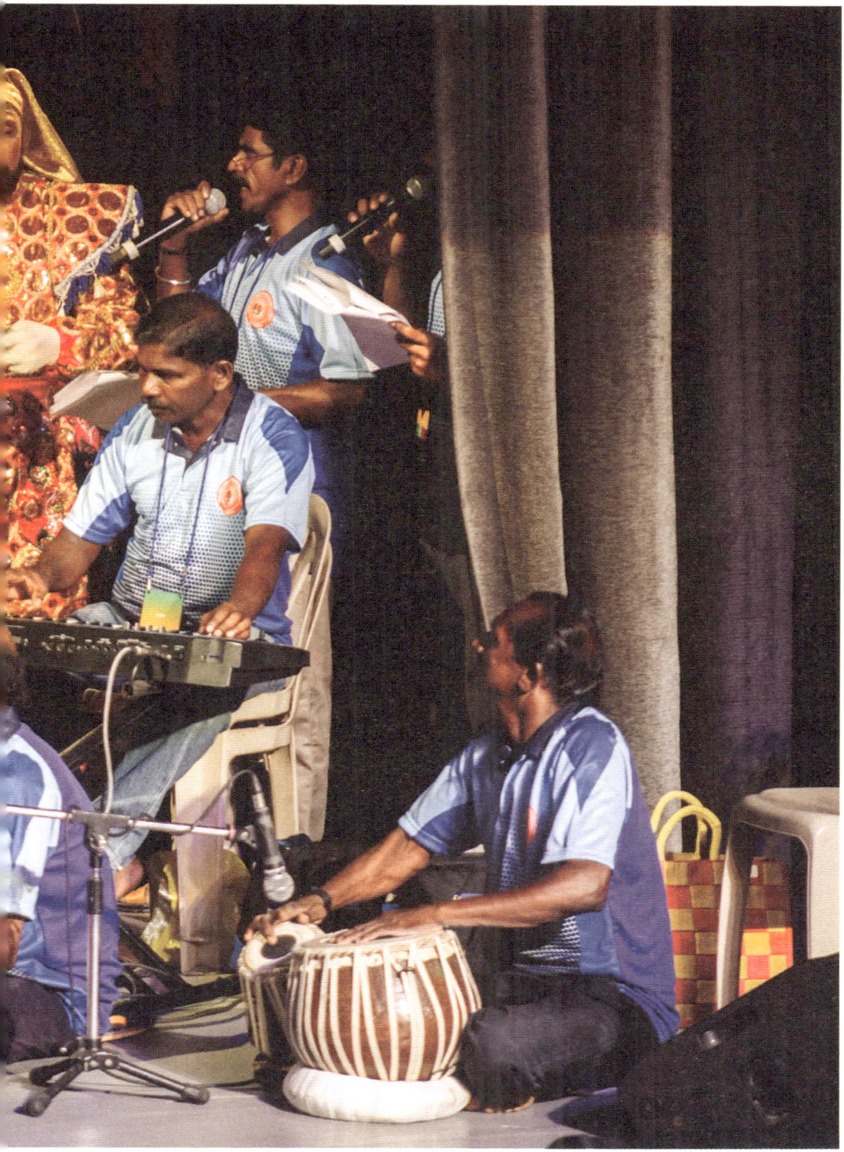

professionalism that instigated into the structure of other folk forms along with exposure. She feels the need to refine the performance and, more importantly, that the performers need to be confident and less insecure about their art. Samson refers to the aestheticisation/professionalism introduced in the performance of Kattaikuthu[13] as the form began thriving in other performance spaces. When I asked Thambi Payyampilly about the changes that he might wish to bring into the form, he clarified that the movements and music will continue to provide the framework while new narratives can be introduced. The idea of refinement has not affected the performance of Chavittu Nadakam so far.

Through my little involvement with Gothuruth, I think it is not the aesthetic quality of the art that retained the form, but it is the emotion and identity associated with it. There are other groups outside Gothuruth which are more interested in "improving" the choreography of the form. One should be certain of the cultural setting of the practice that creates the stage and viewership of Chavittu Nadakam while corresponding with the idea of "refining" it according to the contemporariness of time and space. The way people receive and lived the form changes everything that matters about it. For me, transfiguring a form according to our aesthetics by disengaging with its cultural environment is a process of defacement. We, the institutionalised art public, tend to criticise art forms for their "shortfalls," but is it ethical to denigrate a form in order to "reform" it?

Notes

[1] The Saint Thomas Christians, also called Syrian Christians, are a community among the Christians of Kerala, who trace their origins to the evangelistic activity of Thomas the Apostle in the 1st century. According to them, Thomas the Apostle (Saint Thomas), who is said to have brought Christianity to India, came to the coast of Kerala and converted some people to Christianity.

[2] The Synod of Diamper, held at Udayamperoor, was a diocesan synod or council that laid down rules and regulations for ancient Saint Thomas Christians of the Malabar Coast, the council that revived and Romanised the Kerala church from existing belief system that followed traditional rituals and beliefs of Kerala. The Portuguese missionary Aleixo de Menezes who became the Archbishop of Goa was the leader of The Synod of Diamper of Udayamperoor. The diocesan insisted on accepting the superiority of the Pope of Rome over all other authorities. During the council many local customs were demolished, and they even burnt the manuscripts of local traditions and religious texts of Saint Thomas Christians. There have been poetic narratives written instead of Pana—a ritual form of a vocal genre —as *Puthanpana* (new pana), which narrate the story of Christ. It cleared the way for the Portuguese to forcefully implement their customs, superiority, regulations, mass and rites among Saint Thomas Christians. There are Christian groups in Kerala who believe that the acts of the diocesan council killed Kerala Christian culture, which is multitudinous in nature, and socially the Synod of Diamper has long-term impact among Christian communities in Kerala.

[3] Sabeena Rafi, *Chavittu Nadakam* (Kochi: Pranatha Books, 1980), 48. Most of the quotes used in this article are loose translations of Malayalam books and interviews.

[4] N. P. Unni, "Vyangyavyakhya," in *Margi Souvenir*, ed. by D. Appukkuttan Nair (Trivandrum: Margi Theatre Publications, 1976), 41–53.

[5] Jonas Thaliath, *The Synod of Diamper* (Rome: Pont. Institutum Orientalium Studiorum, 1958) 152-153.

[6] Fr. Valiyaveettil, V. T. J., *Chavittu Nadakam: Sahithyavum Sangethavum* (Thrissur: Kerala Sahitya Akademi, 2011), 37.

[7] Valiyaveettil, *Chavittu Nadakam: Sahithyavum Sangethavum*, 26.

[8] Joly Puthussery, "*Chavittunatakam*: Music-Drama in Kerala," *Comparative Drama* 37, No. 3/4 (Fall/Winter 2003-2004): 337.

[9] Rafi, *Chavittu Nadakam*, 29.

[10] Rafi, *Chavittu Nadakam*, 163.

[11] Uttara Asha Coorlawala, *Classical and Contemporary Indian Dance: Overview, Criteria and A Choreographic Analysis* (New York: New York University Press, ProQuest, 1995).

[12] Yvonne Rainer, "From an Indian Journal," *The Drama Review* 15, No. 2, Theatre in Asia (Spring 1971): 132.

[13] *Kattaikuthu* is another name of *Terukuthu* but P. Rajagopal and Hanne M. de Bruin started an institute for the training of the form and they began emphasising the name *Kattaikuthu*. Through the institute and regular performances outside, *Kattaikuthu* become 'stylistically adapted' to the urban theatre setting. Nowadays, P. Rajagopal and his team collaborate with classical singers like T N Krishna, and this is named as *Karnatic Kattaikuthu*. There are a number of criticisms against the institute for changing the name and patronising the form.

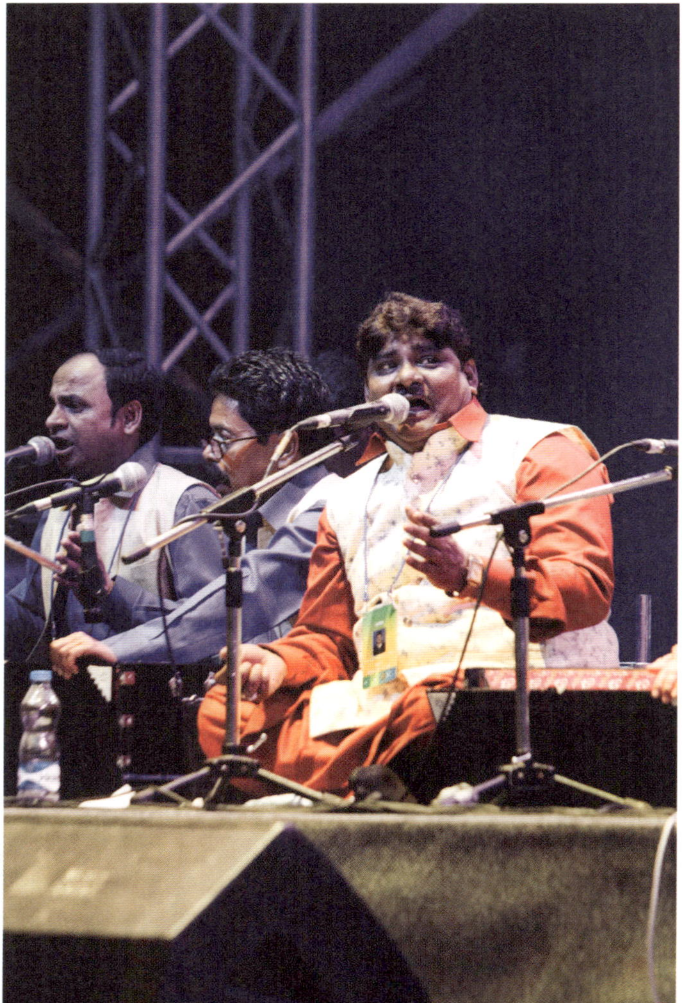

All images from the performance of *Songs of Nature*, performed on DB Ground at Serendipity Arts Festival, 2018.

Songs of Nature

Curated by Aneesh Pradhan

Venue DB (Football) Ground

Songs of Nature

Baul Performers *Rajib Das, Amit Sur, Sudipto Chakraborty, Rittik Guchait, Satyajit Sarkar, Mriganabhi Chattopadhyay and Kartick Das Baul.*
Qawwals *Danish Husain Budayuni, Shekhu Husain, Ajamal Khan, Tariq Husain, Usman Husain, Irfan Husain, Hunain Nyazi and Vasim Hasan.*
Langas/Manganiyars *Talab Khan, Nihal Khan, Firoz Khan, Dara Khan, Asin Khan, Latif Khan and Mushtak Khan.*
Sound Design *Nitin Joshi* **Light Design** *Harshavardhan Pathak*
Sutradhaar *Yatindra Mishra*
Special Thanks *Govind Ram*
Curator *Aneesh Pradhan*

Through centuries, seasonal and nocturnal-diurnal cycles and individual elements from nature have inspired repertoire in diverse musical traditions in India. Song-texts celebrating seasons like Vasant (spring) and Varsha (monsoon), or those that describe flora and fauna, address nature in all its splendour. They also use this imagery as metaphor and simile to introspect about human existence, the philosophy of life, spiritual pursuit and more. Practitioners of folk and religious music and art or classical music from different regions have recorded their poetic and musical responses to these stimuli. This performance explored the manner in which Qawwals, Bauls of Bengal, and the Langa and Manganiar musician communities of Rajasthan have responded to motifs from nature. The similarities and dissimilarities in their responses to the same stimuli from nature were showcased during the concert. Ensembles led by vocalists highlighted the individual peculiarities of each of the three musical traditions.

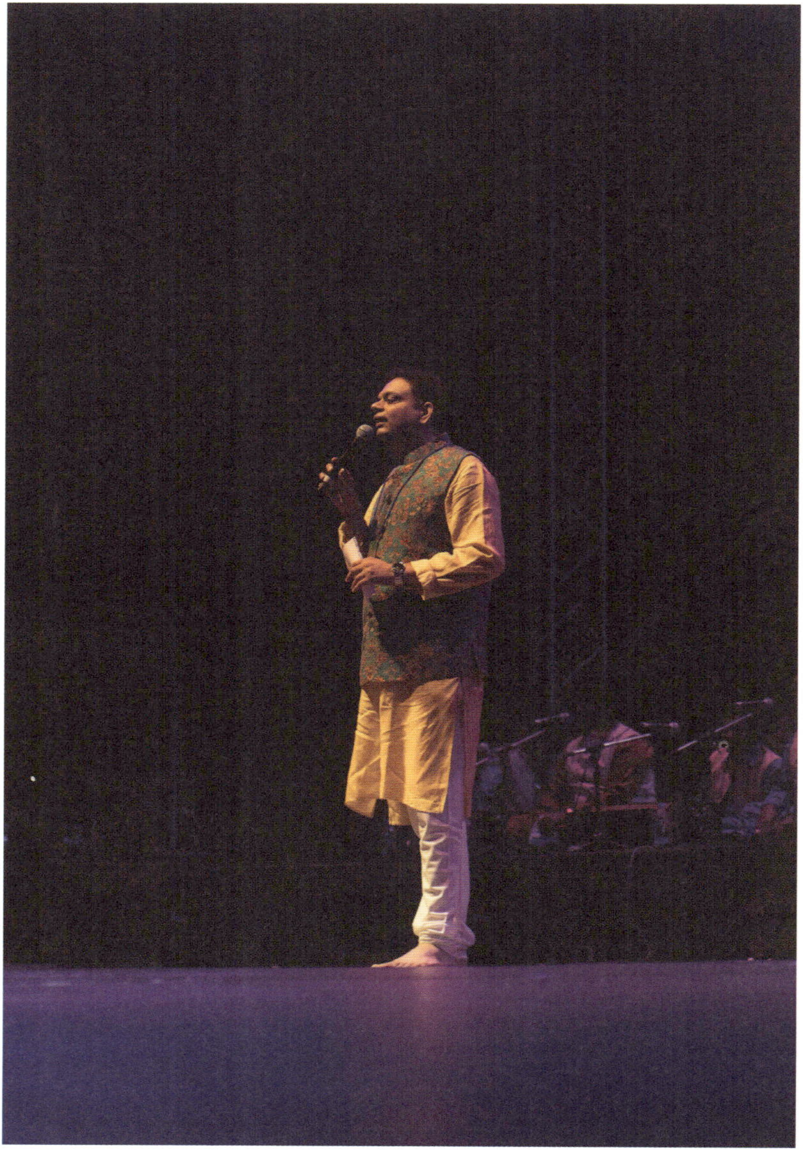

Clouds across a Triptych

AMITAVA SANYAL

"All art constantly aspires towards the condition of music."[1] In saying so, Victorian art critic Walter Pater was making a somewhat straightforward point: art seeks to reduce the distance between form and matter, and music can rise above specific references to do that more effectively than the other arts. Pater was mostly addressing the classical arts seen and heard in Europe in late nineteenth century. What if language muddies the musical matter, as it often tends to do in folk music? After all, the same melody, given different lyrics, may elicit different emotions, or what Pater calls "pure perception." So would folk forms, which are often moored fast with words that speak for a community, struggle to glide form and matter closer to each other? On a more specific performative scale, can folk singers from different linguistic traditions collaborate to produce something that is more than the sum of the parts?

These questions were essential for Aneesh Pradhan, the musician, scholar and publisher who brought together three folk troupes at Serendipity Arts Festival to perform along the theme, *Songs of Nature* (2018). After choosing the three forms represented by the Langas and Manganiyars from western India, Qawwals from north-central India and Bauls from eastern India, Pradhan got to the task of hewing one from the three. He requested the artists to think through the theme. "They sent me some songs and I selected—musically and by narratives. I asked for some more ... That process went on for some time," Pradhan told me.

One of the main things Pradhan was looking at while curating was whether the words rose above the specific and the local—whether they could denote something more universal. "They may come from a tradition and may be singing the songs, but sometimes the metaphors linked to them may not be apparent to them. Is crossing a river just that? Or can it signify a life crossing, or reaching a guru?" And through this search over months, the ubiquity of nature in Indian folk traditions was obvious. It is, after all, the music of the land—a land bearing some of the most bounteous riches of nature nurtured by rains over millenniums.

NATURE'S CONSTANT: CHANGING TASTES AND TONGUES

We live in the Meghalayan Age. Scientists tell us that this stage started about 4,200 years ago when there was a dramatic turn in climate. In South Asia, the monsoon rainfall that greened the land weakened sharply. Geologists found proof of this climatic change in Meghalaya, situated in the Northeastern region of India, amid layers of stalagmites growing on the floor of a cave.[2] And the new slice of the planet's geological time got its name.

This dramatically changed life on the subcontinent. As the western reaches got drier, people migrated eastwards along the Gangetic basin.[3] Towards the end of the first millennium before the Common Era, the Gangetic plain became one of most densely populated parts of the world and a thriving melting pot of cultures. Music struck roots in this fertile land as languages evolved. Congregations, festivals and music were marked by the bi-annual sowing and harvesting cycles, which was the heart of all economic life. The essential feature that defined those cycles was monsoon rainfall.

Theories of music evolved under the broad shade of performance theories. In the thirteenth century, Sarangadev published the *Sangeetratnakara*, a treatise that proposed a typology of music from doctrines developed in the previous millennium. It marked marga *sangeet* (classical music) as different from desi (provincial, not a strict equivalent of folk).[4] Among the two outward differences between the forms, one was that desi music was considered to have taken off around the middle of the first millennium, whereas *marga* music claimed antiquity from ancient Indian musical theatre. The other was that classical was mostly sung in Sanskrit, whereas provincial was also sung in other local languages. Devotional music derived from and enriched both.

As the singers changed and songs evolved, one thing remained constant: nature's prime place in musical language. Evidence of this is available in the paintings that have sought to depict musical moods or raags over the centuries. Men and women may be drawing the viewer's attention in these frames, but it is nature—lurking purposefully in the form of clouds, lightning, rain, streams, trees, flowers and animals—that defines the mood.

***

In the eighteenth century, folk music began to be classified apart from "art" or classical music for the first time in Europe.[5] As the Enlightenment project gained strength, authorship of artworks was emphasised and copyright laws were enacted. Even in the early decades of such laws, that were more interested in printed texts, authorship of music was contested at times, too. Remarkably, this was still a time when musical inspiration could be legitimately held to have come from celestial beings such as the muses—a thought that still resonates among the proponents of classical music in India.

The emergence of European nation-states necessitated a harder look. Mathew Gelbart suggests that the origins of the eventual classifications of music was rooted in nationalism—the desire to have "our" music versus "theirs." He writes, "Cultural nationalists needed to claim communal property, which eventually included tunes."[6] For example, in England, Scottish music (some of it categorised as "Scotch songs") got a rough shoulder from the establishment as a sort of an uncouth cousin, and was filed more as "unrefined" folk music. Later, as the post-industrial middle class grew across Europe, they demanded a more accessible classical music, and one of the forms that met them halfway was the opera, which clad elementary plotlines in popular baubles of melody.

In the late nineteenth century, a somewhat similar effect manifested in India on a less pervasive scale by two men on a wholly different mission—Vishnu Narayan Bhatkhande and Vishnu Digambar Paluskar took on the grand task of classifying and writing down north Indian classical music for the first time. Theirs too was a nationalist project, but it was a part of the larger self-determination movement set in a colonial context.[7]

On the surface, they were not trying to drive a theoretical wedge between folk and classical; rather, their focus was on modernising Hindustani classical forms in terms of scholarship and performance. But, somewhat like in England, they ended up creating an elitist superstructure of typologies in which the place for popular music shrunk, or was shown up as a lesser form. A few forms such as some Hindu devotional music did make the cut, but the songs of workers—the farmer, the smith or the courtesan—were left outside the purview.

As the country's new middle class found a voice in early twentieth century, their aspirations for social mobility brought a new dynamic between the seemingly rural folk and urban classical. In the early decades, the Gramophone Company recorded various artists starting with Gauhar Jaan, the daughter of a courtesan of Armenian descent. Few of the 600-odd 78 RPM records she cut, or the thousands that others recorded in those early decades, were classified as folk.

A set of independent, modern songs started gaining popularity in towns and cities through records and the theatre, growing into a space that folk forms might have used to reach a wider audience. But folk's connection with audiences stayed strong despite the disregard from the dominant distributors of the time. At concerts, an *ustad* or a *vidushi* would at times perform a folksy *dhun* here, or make a raag of a hilly melody there. A few classical singers would sing ghazals too.

***

In the 1950s, India had just started becoming familiar with the radio, the first true tool of public broadcast that took music to the masses at a scale that was not possible earlier. The newly independent state took over the role of being the principal patron of music from individuals and temples, and from the colonial administration the role of the censor. The harmonium, a European instrument warmly adopted by folk and classical musicians across India, was proscribed on the radio. Film music became wildly popular. But for a while Ceylon Radio became the most popular station in India when All India Radio turned up its nose at film music.

Distribution took another leap in the 1960s, when families started huddling around their own, smaller transistor sets, rather than listening to music drifting in from a neighbour's bulkier radio. All forms of music started getting subsumed into film music, and with All India Radio's Nehruvian mission of making one nation out of diverse sub-nations, Hindi music was promoted more than the regional traditions. A few forms were given a fresh lease of life, but most shrank in a nation forcing homogeneity upon itself.

If there was one factor that remained constant through the centuries, it was the essential context of livelihoods. Even in the 1950s, four out of every five Indian households depended on agriculture to make a living. Even in the era of the modernising Five-Year Plans, most Indians' link to land was clear and present. And in that world, the monsoon rains—which still irrigated most of the arable land—had the pride of place in a popular imagination, as did the seasons involved with harvest cycles.

So while melodies, rhythms, instruments, authorship, patronage

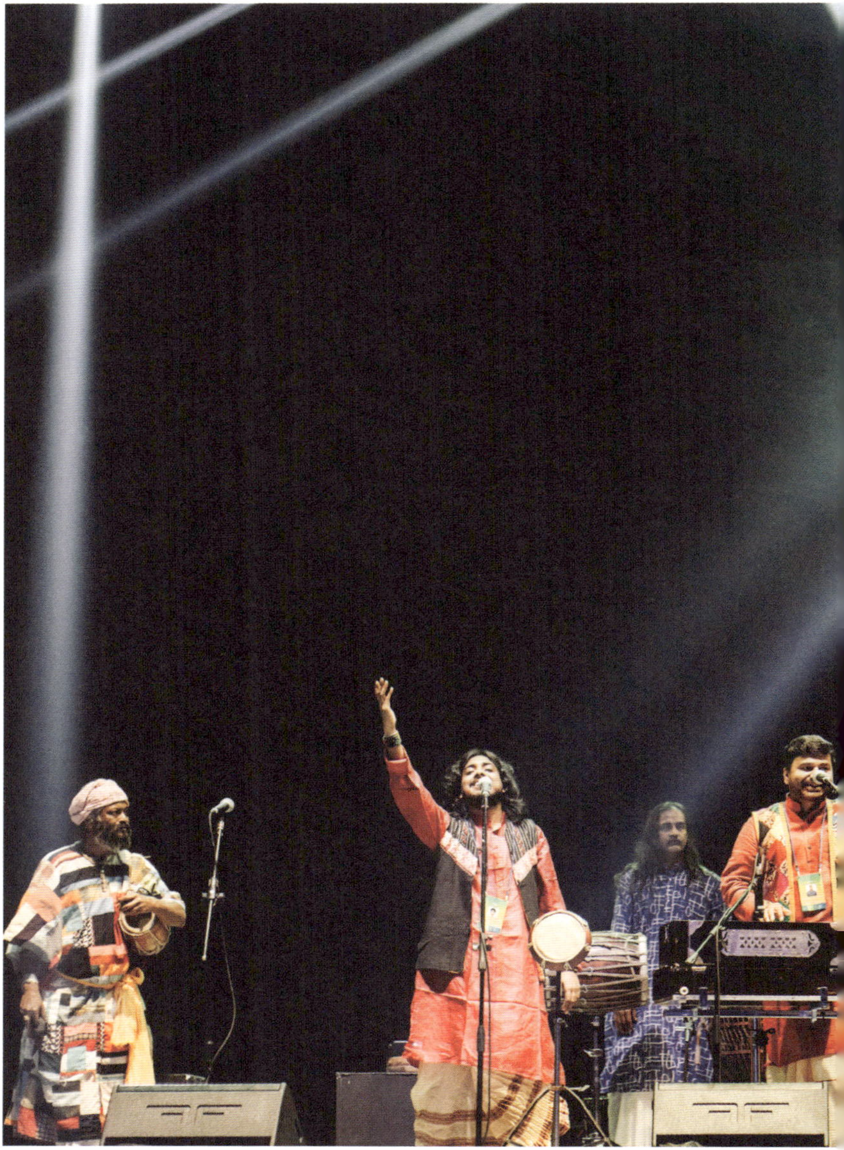

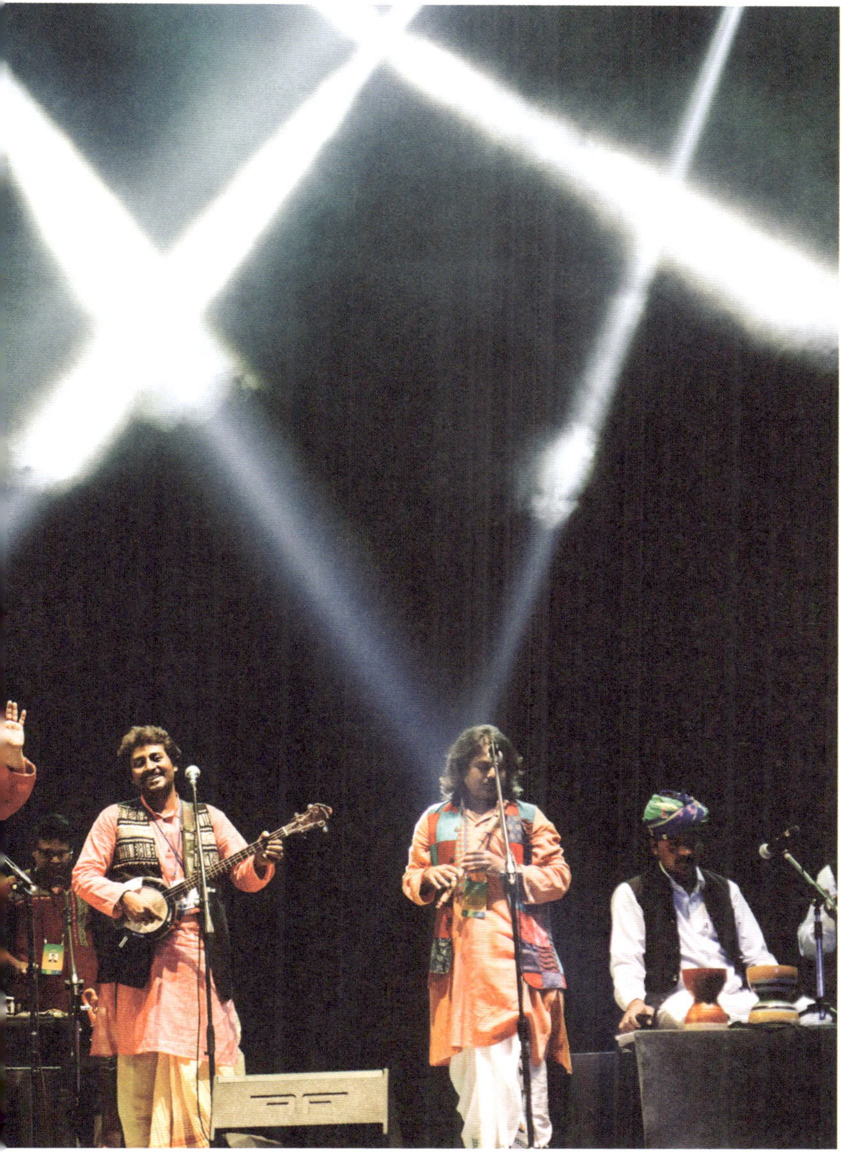

and distribution networks evolved over time, nature's place in music remained central.

THREE FOLK TRADITIONS: DEFINED IN DIVERSITY

Pradhan puts his cards on the table early in our conversations: "I am an irreligious person. But I hold that forces of nature have always been worshipped around the world, whether as fire, water, earth or wind. I am constantly interested in seeing the tangible and intangible manifestations of these, whether in the sagun or nirgun traditions."

With this in mind, Pradhan brought together three troupes of folk musicians from across the subcontinent: Manganiyars and Langhas from Rajasthan, qawwals from Uttar Pradesh, and musicians from (undivided) Bengal devoted to Baul and other traditions. Pradhan says he was guided in his choice by the depth of the traditions, his familiarity with them and with some of the musicians themselves.

Though these groups perform and tour as modern-day bands would, the rich history of their traditions span not only the geography of the subcontinent, but also its history over centuries.

Of the three, the Manganiyars and Langhas claim the greatest antiquity for their music. Govind Singh Bhati, executive producer of Rajasthan International Folk Festival in Jodhpur, says the Manganiyars have been known for their singing as far back as the seventh century. Though they are identified by their Muslim castes, they personify syncretism by singing songs of both Allah and Krishna. Their patronage, too, has come from both Muslim and Hindu leaders of their regions, among them the current titular king of Marwar, Gaj Singh.

Allegiance to the patron, or *jajman*, is so strong that a musician would need to take his permission to perform for someone else. But the responsibility of their regular livelihood was shared more broadly. Till the nineteenth century, Govind Singh says, it was considered the duty of the tax collector or *thakur* of every village where Manganiyars lived to provide a part of the collected income for those families. Even those in the community who were not musically gifted were taken care of. Today the Langhas are spread across three districts of western Rajasthan and the Manganiyars across five.

Komal Kothari, a scholar of Rajasthani music who has worked closely with the Manganiyar and Langha communities over four decades of ethnographic research and was responsible for taking their music to international audiences, noted that within these castes are sub-castes linked to specific functions.[8] And those roles were handed down generations just as other livelihood skills would be passed along. Women would be taught the music too and perform at village functions, but they would rarely travel to cities to perform. Kothari said that "the transmission of knowledge [among Manganiyars] is of a kind where nothing is taught, yet something is learned."[9]

Govind Singh points out that within the communities they would often call in a better singer or instrumentalist, or one whose repertoire is wider: "They support each other that way even today." Among the troupe brought along by Govind Singh is Nihal Khan, a visually impaired singer with a high pitch, who is respected in the community more for his repertoire more than for the presence of his voice.

***

Qawwali took root almost a millennium ago as a musical form performed in the khanqahs (gathering areas or courtyards of Sufi pirs) of Sufi saints. The khanqah most recognised for its music was that of the thirteenth-century master, Nizamuddin Auliya of Delhi, whose student Amir Khusrau was a prolific composer of qawwalis and its first great poet.

Nizamuddin was called to the courts of various sultans of Delhi on one pretext or another; he routinely avoided appearing in person and communicated through students such as Amir Khusrau. Except on one occasion, when he is said to have stood in the court of Ghiasuddin Tughlaq in front of hundreds of scholars, gathered from across the Islamic world, to defend the rightful place of *mausiqi* or music in Islam.[10] This was—and still is—one of the most contentious questions at the cultural heart of Islam. That day, Nizamuddin prevailed despite the opposition of most of the ulema present, and the sultan allowed music to continue at his khanqah. In the centuries that followed, qawwali flourished as a musical form to bring people closer to god, and became stratified into a performance structure.[11]

Nizamuddin is also said to have instructed Khusrau to write in languages and on subjects close to his listeners' hearts. As Persian made way for more Hindavi (early Hindi), nature too occupied a larger space. More prayers were sent out for rains to drench the scorched earth, or poems composed for a beloved who had gone to her parents' for the harvest season.

For a few decades in the middle of the twentieth century, the mainly devotional form found a new life in a secular stream—for proclaiming earthly love in Hindi films. Composers such as Naushad, Roshan, Laxmikant-Pyarelal and RD Burman worked with lyricists Sahir Ludhianvi, Shakeel Badayuni, Shevan Rizvi and Kaifi Azmi to breathe new life in this sub-genre. Many of these songs were sung by women, which was another first in a deeply patriarchal cultural tradition. Today, though composers such as AR Rahman have employed the "filmy" qawwalis, the form has fallen back into the devotional fold.

However, qawwali has continued being patronised at khanqahs. The troupe leader, Danish Hussain Badayuni, tells me that today, in his state of Uttar Pradesh alone, different schools of qawwali are practised in Rampur, Faizabad, Lucknow, Farrukhabad and Kanpur—apart from his own town of Badayun, the birthplace of Nizamuddin Auliya. But Hussain was not born into any of these qawwal families; he is from the proud Rampur-Sahaswan gharana of Hindustani music, and is a grandson of Ustaad Nissar Hussain Khan.

Hussain's style and repertoire reflect his diverse training—laid on a classical base, with a *gayaki ang* often inspired by *tappas*, and an aversion to the higher pitches that many of his peers consider essential. He is not moored to a particular Sufi order, having been influenced by the likes of Aziz Miyan, Shah Niyaz Ahmad and Mubarak Khan of Bareilly, apart from masters of the Chishti Sufi order.

"In my family, we were warned that if we didn't learn the raags well, we'd be given away to qawwals," Hussain says with a laugh. So how did he fall in with this group? It was his elder brother Wajahat Hussain Khan who broadened the niche of qawwali in the family and nurtured the form. What made it acceptable to him and his family? The trail blazed by Nusrat Fateh Ali Khan. What about the filmy qawwalis? "You tell me, how can women sing qawwali? They were not being true to the form."

It so happened that none of the three folk troupes at the festival had women, though each tradition has and has had women who are masters of the form.

***

Qawwali also informs the folk music of the corner of Bengal that inspires Rajib Das. Das and the late Kalika Prasad Bhattacharya, the original founder of their band Dohar (meaning choir or having two parts—signifying the two Bengals to the band), were college-mates who were attracted to the creative variety in the music of Sylhet or Srihatta district, now in north-eastern Bangladesh.

The biggest influence on the district's music is the fourteenth-century Sufi pir, Shah Jalal. Das says Shah Jalal, born in Turkey of Persian descent, first landed in the subcontinent on the west coast. His journey up to the coast, and then through the rugged heartland of Maharashtra, Madhya Pradesh and the Chhotanagpur plateau before reaching the fertile river-fed Sylhet, informed the melodies and

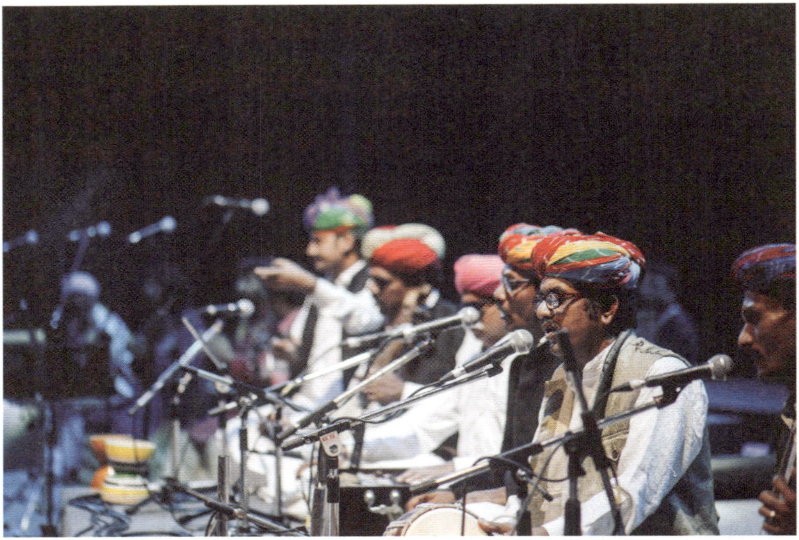

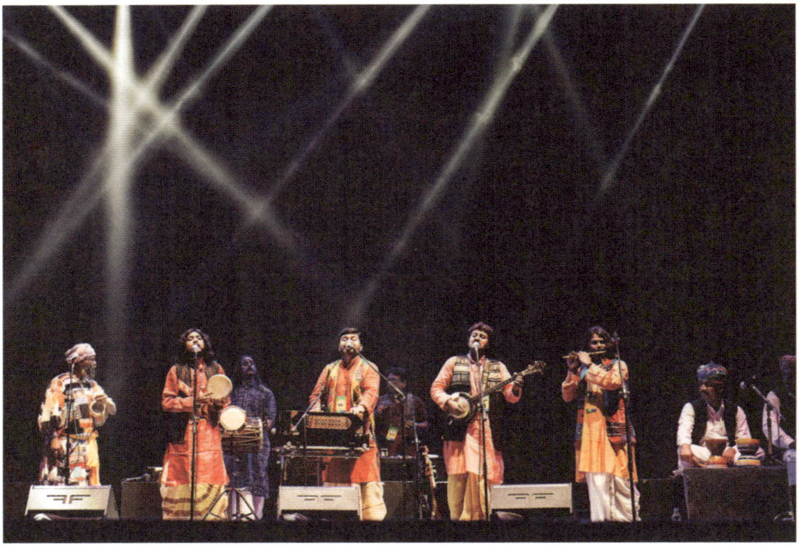

rhythms he brought to the region. Shah Jalal also sowed the seeds of a form of syncretism that has survived the challenge of time—a culture that was nurtured in Sylhet in the twentieth century by songwriter Shah Abdul Karim.

Today, Das and his crew continue to collect folk music and bring to audiences some lesser heard styles or compositions, from the Sufi fakiri, Vaishnav kirtan, Bhawaiya and jhumur traditions, among others. For Serendipity Arts Festival, they were banded together by Pradhan with Kartik Das, a Baul who sings the songs of Bengal's minstrels.

Unlike the other two troupes, members of the Bengali group were not pushed by their families to make a profession of music. While Rajib Das dreamed of forming a band in college, a pre-teen Kartik was initiated as a Baul when a French film crew took him along to be ordained by his would-be guru, Debdas Baul, as the subject of a documentary; he stayed with his guru for 11 years, after which he started busking on trains and eventually performing on stage.

Bauls claim their cultural lineage from the twelfth-century Vaishnav poet Jaydev, writer of the *Gita Govinda*. Apart from some Vaishnav sects, they have been influenced over time by Sufism, Tantrism and Nathpanthis. Modern-day practitioners like Kartik Das would sing songs composed by the nineteenth-century Muslim fakir Lalon Shah as much as those by the twentieth-century Kali devotee Bhaba Pagla.

Unlike the meagre but assured patronage for the Manganiyars, Langhas and qawwals, most Bauls were persecuted for centuries and driven from villages until recently. Their characteristic long hair would be forcibly cut, their dotaras (originally two-stringed, now usually four-stringed instruments) would be broken. In West Bengal, they are today clustered mostly in three districts.[12]

So the three folk forms selected by Pradhan are all different in their centuries-old traditions passed down familial or preceptor-student lines. Apart from some similarities in some melodic structures, the use of some instruments and a preponderance of nature, perhaps the most essential philosophical similarity between them is their exhortation to search within one's mind and body the answers one seeks out in the world.

THE PROCESS OF PERFORMANCE: MAKING ONE OF THREE

It is now two evenings to go to the festival concert and the three troupes of musicians—all 22 of them—have poured into a long room in the magnificent Menezes Braganza Institute by the Mandovi River in Panaji. Pradhan is rushing to meet the musicians for the first rehearsal. As he and I bound up the stairs, we can hear dholak beats bouncing off the old walls and one of the troupes giving full throat to a song. The curator's entrance puts the brakes on the performance. Cold introductions melt into warm smiles as more tea is poured.

The curator's job here is not easy—packed into the room are egos born of centuries of tradition, confidence hardened with decades of public performances, and basic differences in languages and backgrounds. None of the troupes have met or heard the others before. And they all have to click as one ensemble on stage in two days.

Pradhan first wins it with laughter and humility. As the rehearsal gets underway, he suggests something simple that goes a long way in bringing everyone to the same level. Till now, the musicians were sitting across from each other at various heights. Pradhan requests everyone to sit on the ground, facing the same direction. The faint edge of competitiveness or indifference bordering on passive aggression is snuffed out of the room. The musicians' professionalism and genuine appreciation of each other's craft take over.

Would Pradhan ask a musician to cross ranks and play with another troupe? "That's not something I can or would like to force on them. It's wonderful if it happens—but it will have to be up to the musicians themselves," he says. Sure enough, as the electricity of music crackles in the room, the Rajasthani player of the khartal (rhythm device similar to castanet), a most mischievous of instruments, joins in for one of the qawwalis.

All this while sound engineer Nitin Joshi, a key member of Pradhan's team whose job it is to bring the various timbres, pitches and sound levels to comparable levels, is darting around the room and making elaborate notes on sitting arrangements, the microphones needed, and the instruments to be played. What is the secret of his success for making such an ensemble work? "The technical bit is something straightforward—if changes need to be made, I'll try to explain it to them as it is. But then there is the ego bit; a large part of my job is to make their egos agree to the changes I want, or telling them that what they want may not be possible."

Another layer of complexity is added to Joshi's job by the uniqueness of at least one instrument in each group. The defining sound of the Manganiyars comes from the kamaicha (apart from the khartal), a bowed instrument with three main strings and 14 jhara or resonating strings made of copper and steel. Its plaintive tone is a kaleidoscopic mirror of the human voice.

The warm sound of the Bengali Baul's two-stringed khamak or gubgubi, on the other hand, emanates these days from badminton gutting strings. The oculiform plectrum, often called chokh or eye, can be used to mark the rhythm or, in the hand of a master like Kartik Das Baul, shepherd the melody section.

The unique sound of a qawwali troupe comes from the clapping of hands in unison. This rhythmic repetition, which might induce a trance-like effect in a distant listener, can transport a believer to rapture.

A common instrument between the three forms is the dholak. Here, too, there are differences, notes Pradhan: "The rope-strung dholak's sound is slightly different from that of those tightened with a steel rim and nuts ... Though most of the songs are in the kaharwa and dadra taals, they are phrased differently in the three styles, with different stresses."

The most crucial meeting ground has to be the availability of songs from each repertoire that fit the overall theme and can be strung together into separate sub-themes. "I want to see whether any song texts mentioning aspects of nature have meanings on another plane rather than just the immediate. I want to know what inspired the text," says Pradhan. "Is a river just a river, as mentioned in song, or is the song trying to say something more, something deeper?"

He notes that while all the traditions have songs on *basant* and *baarish* (the spring and rain), it is not surprising that the musicians from the arid western Rajasthan have little about rivers or flowers. Even within the Bengali folk traditions, the Bauls of Rarh, or the red-soil region of western Bengal, have fewer songs of rain than those of the other, more rain-washed parts of Bengal. Even achingly beautiful songs have to be kept aside because they do not belong in the theme. Where consensus is elusive, cajoling and the curator's call are used. Songs are chopped up and bits are added to other songs to make the mix fall into the groove. Performances are timed and trimmed into allotted slots, so that the whole adds up to approximately 90 minutes.

Over the next two-and-a-half days, four clear sub-themes emerge: basant, baarish, nadi and pakshi (spring, monsoon, rivers and birds), to be presented in that order. Several songs selected in the latter two sub-themes pass Pradhan's test of making sense on a metaphysical level too. Rivers are flows of life and rowing to the other bank more momentous than merely crossing over; birds fly high with the deepest desires beyond clouds of reason.

The last thread in making one performance out of the three sets of performers is Yatindra Mishra, the *sutradhar* or compère for the evening. A poet and historian of music from Ayodhya, Mishra entranced the crowd with his mix of *khadi* and *mithi boli* (Urdu and Hindi parlance of Braj). It all seemed seamless—every performance was like a piece of crafted metal which Mishra would melt with his Ganga-*Jumni tehzeeb* (civility born of the Ganga-Yamuna basin) to cast into the mould of the next performance.

A visual sense of balance was conveyed with the Bengali group standing in the middle and the other two sitting on platforms on either side. The evening started with an Amir Khusrau composition, “Aj racho Basant Nizam ghar” (Let spring bloom in Nizamuddin’s house today). And then a cue was passed around the stage by Mishra. As musical energy flitted right to left and left to right on the stage, the folk groups’ infectious rhythms and earthy melodies convinced the audience of the depth of their lived traditions.

For the final song, “Aane de badal kale” (Let the black clouds come), sung by Danish Hussain and his group, Pradhan moved from the front of the stage to the wings, and implored the other two troupes to join in. And the carefully woven garland of songs was tossed up into the evening air with a finishing flourish.

***

“*Raag, rasoi aur pagdi*” (Singing a raag, cooking a dish, and tying a turban), Danish Hussain says with relish, get done to satisfaction only at times. So did the final performance of *Songs of Nature* satisfy all the collaborators? Did the triptych present a unified picture? The musicians themselves think it did. The Sunday crowd at DB Ground seemed to enjoy it too, by all accounts. But whether the concert as a whole transcended the literal or exceeded the sum of its performances, the theme bears repetition. More than four millennia after a truly earth-shaking climatic event, we are facing another form of life-threatening change. If *Songs of Nature* reminded us of what we need to nurture in the near future, it would have served a lofty purpose.

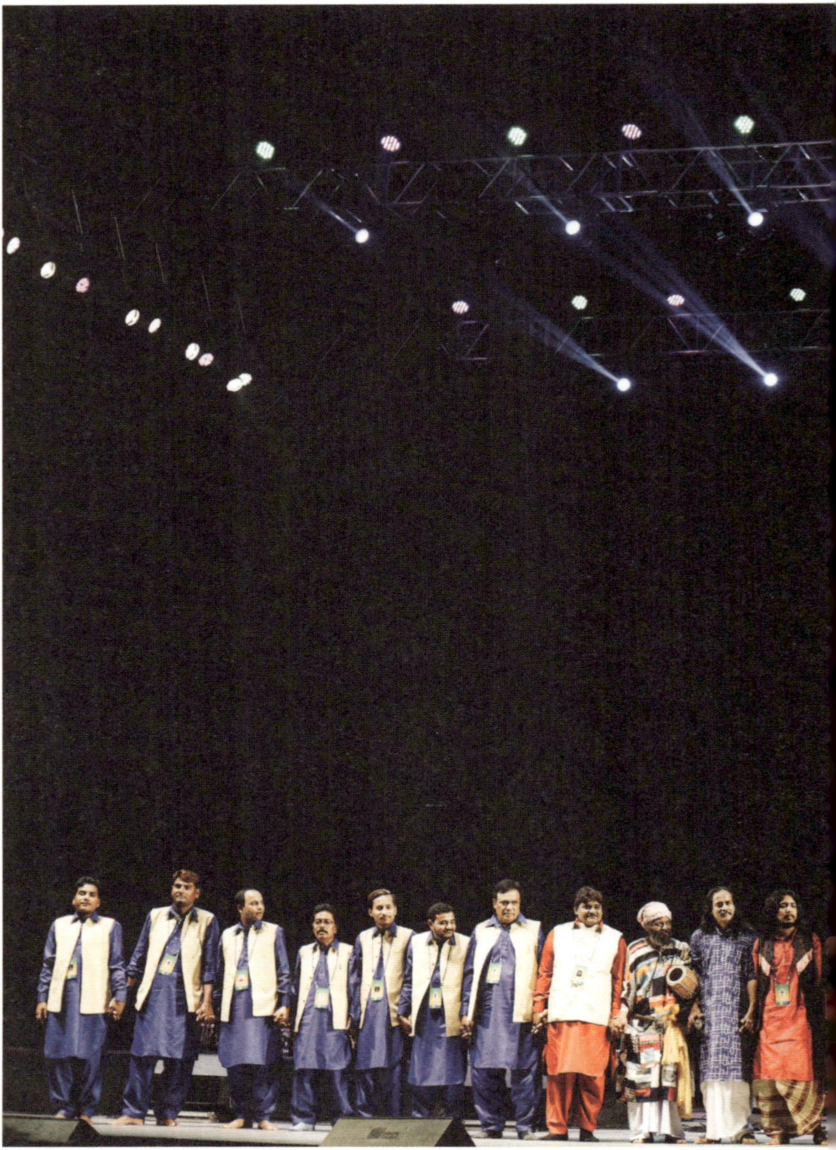

Notes

[1] Walter Horatio Pater, "The School of Giorgione," *The Renaissance: Studies in Art and Poetry, 1877, accessed at The Renaissance: Studies in Art and Poetry: A Victorian Web-book*, http://www.victorianweb.org/authors/pater/renaissance/7.html

[2] Jonathan Amos, "Welcome to the Meghalayan Age – a new phase in history," BBC News, published on 18 July 2018, https://www.bbc.com/news/science-environment-44868527

[3] Peter D Clift, R. Alan Plum, *The Asian Monsoon: Causes, History and Effects* (Cambridge: Cambridge University Press, 2008); Romila Thapar, *The Penguin History of Early India* (London: Penguin Books, 2003).

[4] Lewis Rowell, *Music and Musical Thought in Early India* (London: University of Chicago Press, 1992).

[5] Mathew Gelbart, *The Invention of 'Folk Music' and 'Art Music': Emerging Categories from Ossian to Wagner* (Cambridge and New York: Cambridge University Press, 2007).

[6] Gelbart, *The Invention of 'Folk Music' and 'Art Music': Emerging Categories from Ossian to Wagner*, 24.

[7] Janaki Bakhle, *Two Men and Music: Nationalism in the Making of an Indian Classical Tradition* (Oxford and New York: Oxford University Press, 2005).

[8] Rustom Bharucha, *Rajasthan, an Oral History: Conversations with Komal Kothari* (New Delhi: Penguin Books, 2003).

[9] Bharucha, *Rajasthan, an Oral History: Conversations with Komal Kothari*, 232.

[10] Tanvir Anjum, *Chishti Sufis in the Sultanate of Delhi, 1190-1400: From*

Restrained Indifference to Calculated Defiance (New Delhi: Oxford University Press, 2011).

[11] Regula Burckhardt Qureshi, *Sufi Music of India and Pakistan: Sound, Context and Meaning in Qawwali* (Cambridge: Cambridge University Press, 1986).

[12] Shaktinath Jha, *Baul-Fakir Dhongsher Andolcner Itibritta* (Kolkata: Subarnarekha, 2001).

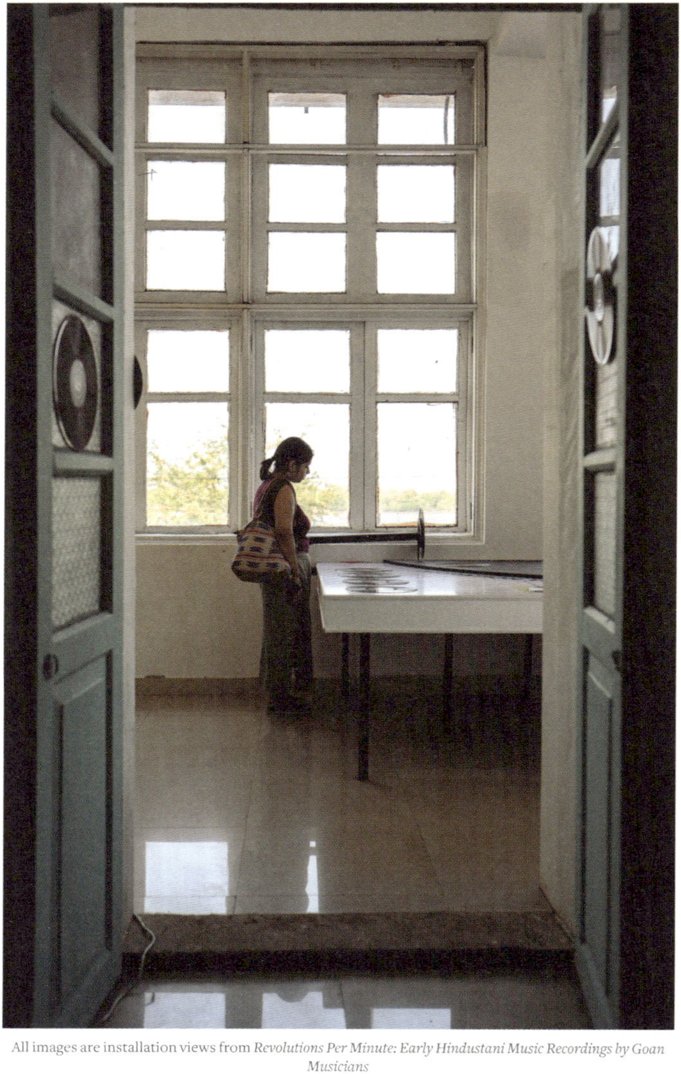

All images are installation views from *Revolutions Per Minute: Early Hindustani Music Recordings by Goan Musicians*

Revolutions Per Minute: Early Hindustani Music Recordings by Goan Musicians

Curated by Aneesh Pradhan

Venue Old GIM

Curatorial Note

Curated by *Aneesh Pradhan*
Design and Layouts by *Pushkar Thakur*
Collaborator *Dr. Suresh Chandvankar*
Exhibition Design and Layout *Pushkar Thakur*

Until the mid-nineteenth century, royal courts in India were the main source of patronage to Hindustani music. But after 1858, the establishment of the British Crown as the paramount power in India crippled Indian princely power. This seems to have led to a sharp decline in royal patronage to Hindustani music, the art or classical music tradition of North India, but for a few last vestiges. In the absence of sustained support from royal patrons and the colonial government, musicians identified the Indian commercial, industrial and intellectual elite present in colonial cities as prospective patrons. Gradually, hereditary musicians and courtesans from Northern and Central India migrated to Bombay (now officially called Mumbai), one of the most important colonial cities in India.

Musicians migrating to Bombay included women of the devadasi community from Goa and neighbouring areas, who were engaged in service to temples. Their migration to Bombay gave them an opportunity to enrich themselves musically by training under maestros representing well-known lineages and styles of vocal and instrumental music.

Over time, many of the women and men from these Goan families became celebrated musicians inspiring successive generations. Their music recorded in the first half of the twentieth century on 78 rpm gramophone discs, represents a legacy that continues to be a rich resource for musicians, scholars, students, and listeners. This exhibition showcased the journey of these musicians, particularly their career as performers for the gramophone industry.

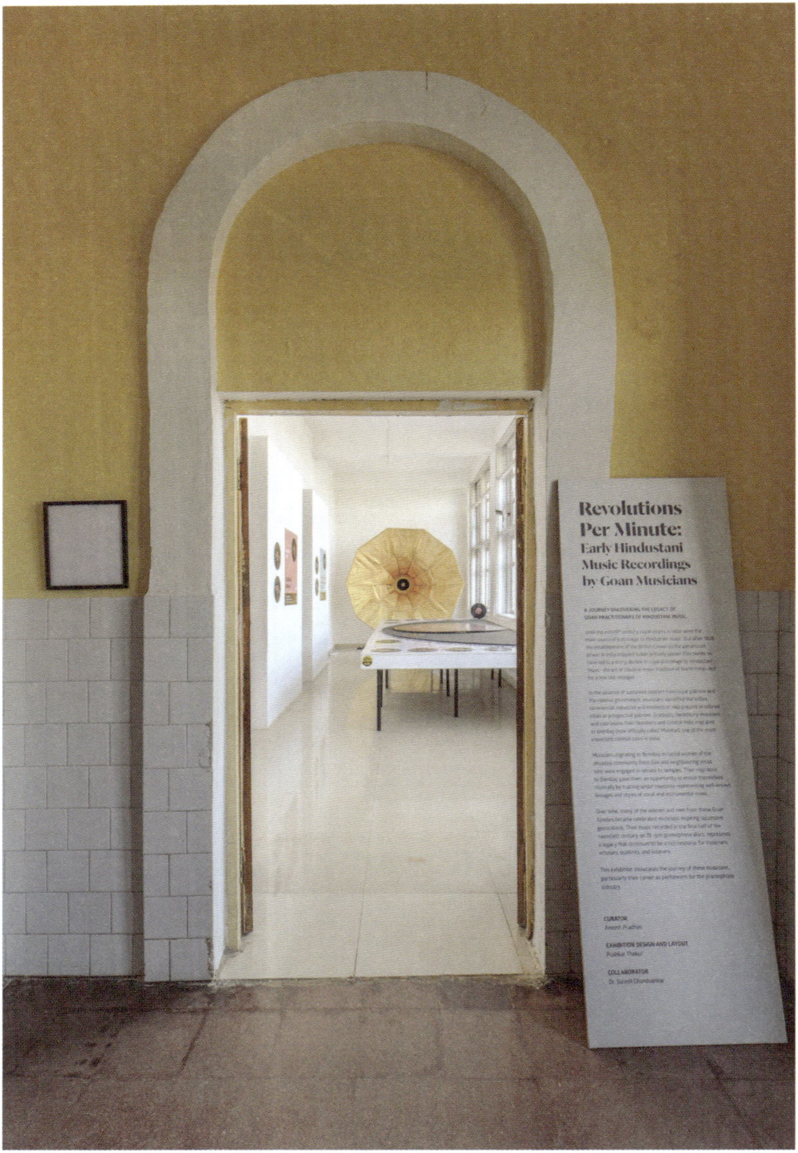
Revolutions Per Minute:
Early Hindustani Music Recordings by Goan Musicians
A JOURNEY UNCOVERING THE LEGACY OF GOAN PRACTITIONERS OF HINDUSTANI MUSIC
CURATOR
EXHIBITION DESIGN AND LAYOUT
COLLABORATOR

The Revolution Might Just Be Phonographed

MAYA PALIT

> Sweeping across the country with the speed of a transient fashion in slang or Panama hats, political war cries or popular novels, comes now the mechanical device to sing for us a song or play for us a piano, in substitute for human skill, intelligence, and soul... From the days when the mathematical and mechanical were paramount in music, the struggle has been bitter and incessant for the sway of the emotional and the soulful. And now, in this the twentieth century, come these talking and playing machines, and offer again to reduce the expression of music to a mathematical system of megaphones, wheels, cogs, disks, cylinders, and all manner of revolving things... Then what of the national throat? Will it not weaken? What of the national chest? Will it not shrink? When a mother can turn on the phonograph with the same ease that she applies to the electric light, will she croon her baby to slumber with sweet lullabys, or will the infant be put to sleep by machinery?... In the prospective scheme of mechanical music, we shall see man and maiden in a light canoe under the summer moon upon an Adirondack lake with a gramophone caroling love songs from amidships. The Spanish cavalier must abandon his guitar and serenade his beloved with a phonograph under his arm.
>
> - John Philip Sousa, *The Menace of Mechanical Music*

We do not need to call John Philip Sousa an alarmist: he admits that himself in his 1906 treatise, "The Menace of Mechanical Music," where the American composer castigates the craze developing around "music-reproducing machines."[1] His list of grievances is longwinded, and it is difficult to swallow, with a straight face, his concern for the loss of the maternal instinct as a byproduct of the phonograph. But from all his handwringing and hyperbole emerges a sense of anxiety, universal at the time, about how mechanical reproduction would alter the landscape of music.

What would become of the soulfulness of live performance? Wouldn't an imitation of a performance pale in comparison to the original? Would the spontaneity of performance be marred by the presence of technology? And wouldn't the ubiquity of recorded music foster a disinclination for learning instruments, leading to a decline in music as an art form and a deterioration in musical capabilities (and chests and throats)?

These apprehensions were echoed wherever the gramophone—Emile Berliner's 1888 invention, a remodeling of Edison's phonograph that replaced cylinders with flat discs—picked up popularity. And although it might be easy to dismiss Sousa from our current standpoint (in a world where technological equipment becoming an appendage to the human body is no longer a mere prospect), the arrival of the gramophone and other musical technology in India in the late-nineteenth and twentieth century evoked similar responses. For instance, All India Radio's somewhat condescending 1955 chronicle of Indian musicians' first interaction with the gramophone and radio, describes their initial reaction as "one of suspicion, vague fear and even contempt at times. They would simply refuse to face the 'mike' which, some apprehended, would permanently swallow their voices; according to others it would rob them of their precious treasure and make it available to others irrespective of their unwillingness or otherwise to part with it. Still others abhorred the idea of their music being heard in hotels, restaurants and shops." [2] Perhaps one of the artists this description referred to was Bade Ghulam Ali Khan, an esteemed Punjabi musician who, according to the writer Namita Devidayal, was convinced that recording equipment would steal the life from his voice and leave him "insipid and impotent."[3]

In December, 2018, as I walked around an exhibition at the Goa Institute of Management, titled *Revolutions Per Minute: Early Hindustani Music Recordings by Goan Musicians*, it was evident that the materials on women singers who had been recorded outnumbered those on their male counterparts. After conversations with the musician and author Aneesh Pradhan, who curated the exhibition for Serendipity Arts Festival in collaboration with the prolific record collector Suresh Chandvankar and the designer Pushkar Thakur, the reasons behind allotting significantly more space to these women became clear.

While fear, nervousness or disconcertment dominated some musicians' initial response to the prospect of being recorded, this technology was also embraced by others. "The idea of the disembodied voice created tension in the musical community," Pradhan told me, adding that there may have been different rationales behind the musicians' uneasiness, including being afraid that their voices would be captured by the new technology, that it conflicted with the spirit of improvisation in their music or that it would threaten their position as the custodians of musical art. "You find that most of the earlier ustads, particularly those associated with princely courts, did not agree readily to being recorded, which is why most of the early recordings are done by professional women performers. They were keener to take advantage of this new format and remarkable in terms of looking ahead."

Surviving evidence, Pradhan added, suggested that women performers were also featured more often than men in concerts at the time, were patronised largely by the Bombay elite and had more financial stability in the fraternity. At the same time, their visibility worked against them too, with their occupation shrouded in stigma. Social reformists in both Calcutta and Madras, for instance, held campaigns against music and dance performances in the

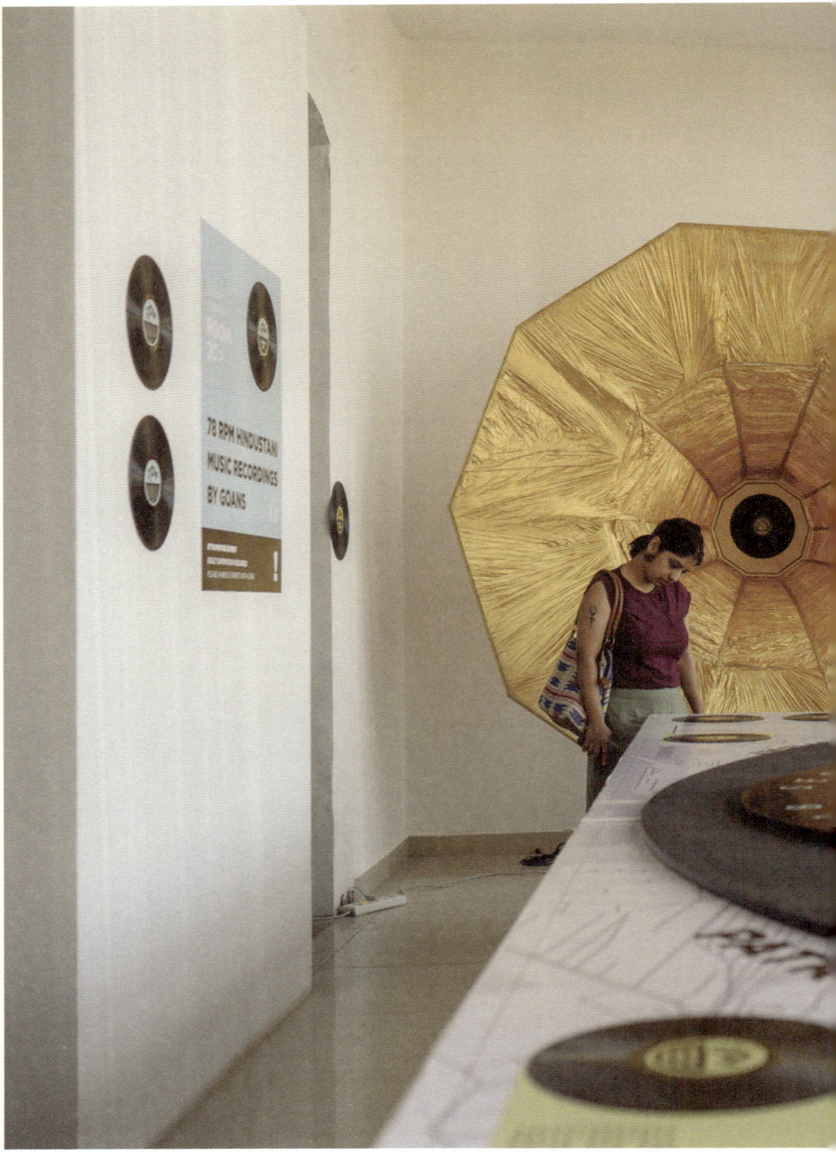
78 RPM HINDUSTANI
MUSIC RECORDINGS
BY GOANS

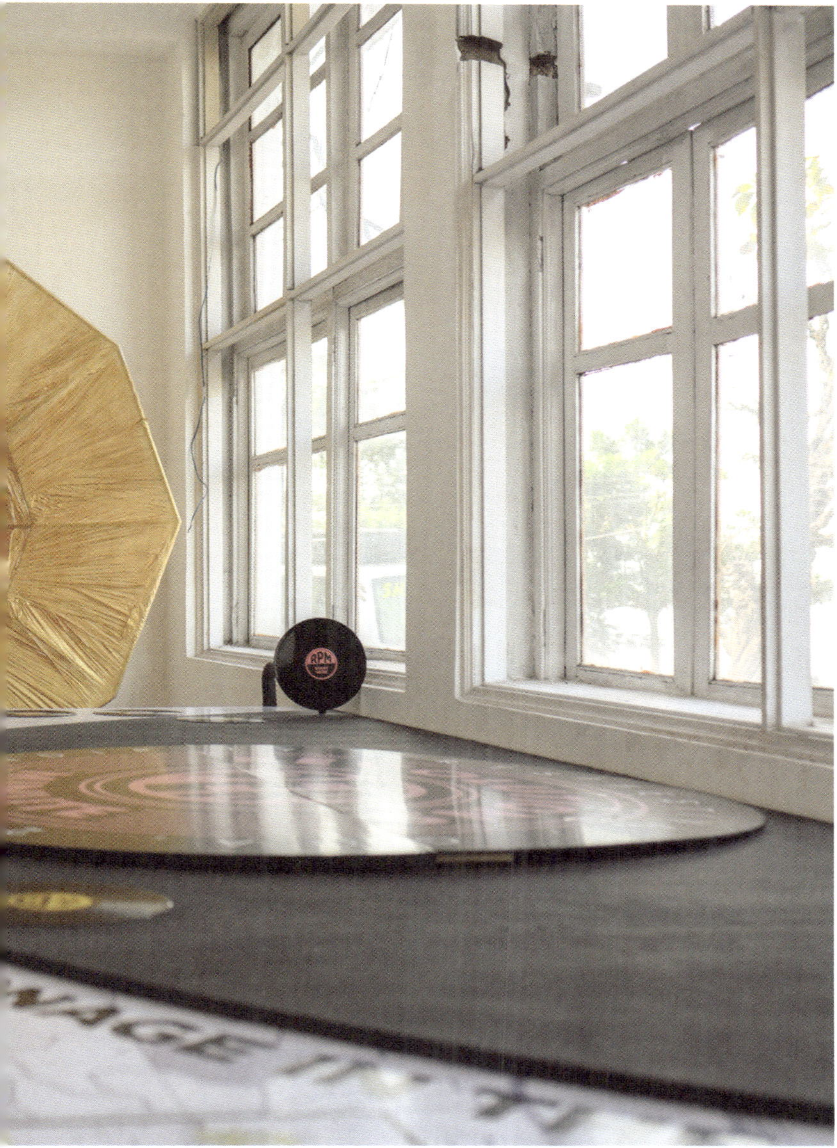

1890s because they were viewed as immoral. A room dedicated to gramophone recordings and associated paraphernalia forms part of the exhibition and serves as a tribute to the enterprising spirit of the performers of the era.

The exhibition was localised in its focus: a historical documentation of Goan musicians' lives and legacies, their migration to Bombay in the late-nineteenth and early-twentieth centuries and the critical role the city played in their trajectories. But its acknowledgement of the milieu in which these musicians worked, and their sense of recording as a transformative phenomenon, conjures up a world that is distant, yet relatable.

As we grapple today with the scale of cultural change initiated by technology, it is telling that none of the fads that Sousa lists with such derision, besides the Panama hat, were "transient fashion." Political war cries and novels are still popular, and, unfortunately for Sousa, so is mechanical music.

PERFORMERS, MIGRATION AND THE CITY

A turntable and a giant gramophone horn made of steel pipes and cling film covering nearly an entire wall was glaringly visible from the entrance to the exhibition. A record was playing, and I spotted large discs labelled "RPM" on the walls and on a table inside the starkly white room. But before I could reach them, the text on a board, leaning against a tiled wall beside the entrance, pulled me away to a different time-frame.

"Until the mid-19th century," the description read, "royal courts in India were the main source of patronage to Hindustani music. But after 1858, the establishment of the British Crown as the paramount power in India crippled princely power." The story of the gramophone in India and its runaway success, these lines seemed to be asserting, is inextricably tied to the period that preceded it.

1858 is spoken of as a convulsing moment in Indian history for its many political developments: a year after the military uprisings and civil rebellions of 1857, the British storming of central Indian states was in full swing and the Queen's Proclamation transferred the governance of India from the British East India Company to the Crown.[4] But for Hindustani music, the year holds significance too, although its effects were more gradually felt.

Up until that point, music appreciation had remained largely the domain of royal courts, including those of Gwalior and Rampur. Although there were stray instances of British support for Hindustani music, according to Aneesh Pradhan's book *Hindustani Music in Colonial Bombay*, these were far and few between. He gestures, tongue-in-cheek, towards the disparaging observations penned by British residents and travelers on Indian musical and dance performances—including a Mrs. Sherwood, who declares that "it is impossible to give any idea of this music... Never before had we heard such fearful screeching and skirling."[5] Moral codes, Pradhan concludes, might have had something to do with the British's aversion to the nature of these performances: "Colonial authors described women performers as 'dancing girls,' equating them with prostitutes and condemning their colleagues as a depraved lot."[6]

The fall of Awadh in 1857, the handover of colonial power in 1858 and the subsequent decline of the princely states led to dwindling support from royal patrons. Since the performers could not rely on the colonial government for endorsement, this initiated a large-scale migration of performers from a variation of musical traditions to cities, as they hunted for new benefactors in the Indian intellectual and commercial elite. However, the scholar Tejaswini Niranjana warns that "the year 1857 is only a symbolic marker" of these shifts, and explains that the slow decline of the Mughal Empire over the eighteenth century had already prompted the dispersal of musicians and courtesans, and created different styles of music in states including Indore, Baroda and Jaipur.[7] Nonetheless, the developments of 1857-58 certainly propelled musicians towards urban centres:

the exile of Wajid Ali Shah, the Nawab of Awadh at the time and a famously ardent patron of music, to Calcutta led to the flourishing of music in the metropolis.[8]

Bombay was the second commercial centre to witness a tremendous influx of musicians. "The city was to Hindustani music in the twentieth century what Delhi had been to it in the sixteenth," the writer Sumana Ramanan concludes, drawing parallels between the celebration of music in Mughal Delhi and in Bombay, three centuries later.[9] Towards the end of the nineteenth century, the city was expanding rapidly and became the hub of private forms of trade, and later, a burgeoning cotton industry. The introduction of railway networks had vastly improved access to the city, and performers from Lucknow, Agra, Gwalior and Hyderabad, as well as Goa, flocked there to teach, attend and perform at concerts, and seek out wealthy patrons. Music schools, clubs, circles and conferences were established in Bombay in the early-twentieth century, after it had become the centre of the recording industry.

It is to be expected, then, that the first room within the exhibition is dedicated to acknowledging the metropolis' centrality to the urbanisation and modernisation of Hindustani music. One of the first things that catches the eye as you enter, after the enormous gramophone horn, is a sprawling map of Bombay. A section of it, labelled "Patronage in the Colonial City," identifies the various parts of Bombay where performers lived. Although, as Pradhan explains at length in his book *Hindustani Music in Colonial Bombay*, there is little evidence to demonstrate how precisely caste divides influenced the organisation of migrant performers' settlements within the city; their places of birth, religions and occupations played a large role in determining the locality in which they resided. Kalbadevi Road and Grant Road were two areas inhabited by performers from the Marwadi, Bene-Israel and Muslim communities, and by Goan women performers, who are within the purview of Pradhan's exhibition.[10] These included women from the *devadasi* tradition, who lived as temple attendants (split along a social hierarchy, they were known variously as *naikins, kavantis* and by other names).[11] Women performers migrating to Bombay also hailed from hereditary courtesan families in northern and central India—known as the *baiji* or *tawaif*, they specialised in *thumri* and *dadra* styles.[12]

"Until the last quarter of the nineteenth century, most of the performances in the cities highlighted solo women acts," Pradhan told me, and suggested that this had something to do with their extensive repertoire gaining popularity among elite audiences as a form of entertainment.[13] Usually conducted in a patron's house, a performance might include many elements, such as a *nach*, involving both singing and dancing, and a *baithak*, or vocal recital. Male musicians at the time, on the other hand, largely relied on teaching and performing with women performers (though by the end of the nineteenth century, affluent businessmen had started to hire them for private concerts, and they later gained centre-stage in the city).[14]

Armed with this context, the contents of the first sub-section of *Revolutions Per Minute* would not be surprising. A smaller room trailing off from the central space with the horn and map, had wall-length discs containing information about four renowned Goan performers of the nineteenth century: Tarabai and Saraswati Bai (known as the Velingkar sisters) from Veling, Bablibai Salgaonkar from Belgaum and Anjanibai Malpekar from Malpe. The discs briefly outlined their trajectories as disciples, with a fact or two about their patrons and the *gharana* or lineage to which their music was affiliated.

The writing and material was sparse for performers such as Bablibai, about whom, as I discovered later, some of the available information, at least about her recording career, is apocryphal or source-based. But certain details on the discs, while seemingly innocuous, emphasised larger connections between their careers and the social environment they inhabited. For instance, although there were no images of the Velingkar sisters, the write-up had an important giveaway, which connects to a fascinating strand of Pradhan's broader research into performance practices at the time: "Though not widely acknowledged, women performers like Tarabai Velingkar also acted as patrons, as they not only engaged male musicians as teachers and accompanists, but also featured them as soloists in soirees that they hosted." The performances at these soirees, or *daavats*, often lasted all night, and they hosted multiple performers who were keen to establish themselves for potential patrons in the audience. According to Pradhan's book, initially "women performers enjoyed a better financial standing in the fraternity"—the main performer of an ensemble received somewhere between thirty and sixty rupees for a single performance at a patron's house, and paid for the accompanists' stay and earnings.[15] By the late-nineteenth century, it was also conventional for well-off women performers to pay monthly fees to the ustads they hired, a tuition of sorts, but the idea of women patrons organising programmes that involved visiting musicians suggests that they were very active in the commercial world of music as well.

Despite this evidence of women performers' agency, the project also provides a window into the fraught gender dynamics and biases that were inescapable for women musicians. The write-up on Anjanibai, who belonged to a family of musicians that migrated to Bombay and established herself as a representative of the Bhendi Bazaar gharana of the sarangi player Nazir Khan, suggests that she adapted her performance style in order to navigate social stigma. It states that it is likely that she decided to stop wearing the *peshwaj*—a costume resembling a long tunic, which was worn by women performers who did both singing and dancing. Drawing on the ethnomusicologist Jennifer Post Quinn's research, Pradhan elaborates on this trend in his book, suggesting that professional women performers were stigmatised by European authors and their work was viewed as synonymous with prostitution. To combat these prejudices, some women performers made certain adjustments—for instance, some attempted to distance themselves from the courtesan tradition by insisting that the word "amateur" was printed alongside their name on records.[16] Pradhan suggests that they may also have chosen to make "a departure from dance that was regarded lascivious or coquettish by reformers," and instead, chose to focus only on singing.[17] He also discusses the possibility that women singers, many of whom were moving away from *thumri* (which included both dance and gesture) towards the *khayal* genre of vocal music, voluntarily abandoned dance in order to "gain equal status with male musicians" and add overtones of "respectability" to their singing performances.

The facts that you can glean from these snippets in the exhibition are critical to forming an understanding of the social conditions under which the performers worked and why their performances mutated in the way they did. This complex history also substantiates the ordering and layers of the exhibition—why, for instance, a work whose title and design suggests it will confine itself to Hindustani musicians recording on 78 RPM begins with performers who were likely to not have been involved in the recording business. Pradhan emphasised over our meetings and correspondence that the chronological sequence was chosen precisely because the histories of these performers help to explain the trajectories of those who came after:

> Bablibai, Velingar, Anjanibai—although they are not recorded, they play an important role because they are part of a generation prior to Kesarbai Kelkar. Had they not migrated to Bombay and made a name for themselves, these later musicians would not have been established. The recording industry and the manner in which musicians ended up recording during this period, did not appear in a vacuum. It all happened in a historical context, and so it was important for me to share this connection with the visitors. We need to know the conditions that led to this migration, the circumstances that they found themselves in as students and performers in Bombay, the possibilities that they had to access patronage, and the manner in which they disseminated their music.

RECORDINGS, COMMERCE, COLONIALISM

The stories of the first gramophone recordings in India are thoroughly amusing in retrospect, partly because they involved unsuspecting gentlemen who were dispatched on colonial "expeditions" to India to collect "native" recordings, and, being unfamiliar with the music, had immense trouble navigating the array of Hindustani musical styles they came up against.[18]

Recordings of Indian music had been carried out in London in 1899 by the Gramophone and Typewriter Limited (GTL), a soon-to-be giant corporation that later, as the Gramophone Company, monopolised the gramophone recording industry for nearly five decades, and eventually created the label, His Master's Voice, or HMV. But until 1901, "talking machines" were sold as musical instruments or curiosos to the affluent classes in India that could afford it, and had not been recognised yet as objects with enormous economic potential because of records that would accompany it. This makes the speed with which the industry expanded over the first decade of the twentieth century all the more startling: by the middle of 1908, the Australian scholar Michael Kinnear estimates, there were more than 10,000 recordings of Hindustani music, encompassing a multitude of styles.[19]

In 1902, an individual named Frederick Gaisberg who worked with the GTL, travelled to Calcutta after much nagging from the company's local agent, Jack Hawd, who incidentally had the good grace to wonder, over one communication, whether it was the most opportune time to kickstart a recording empire, since "12 to 14,000 are dying in this territory weekly now of plague."[20] Gaisberg arrived with pioneering equipment that made it plausible to record duplicates of recorded material.[21] He had designed a motor to do away with the cumbersome batteries and springs formerly used for recording machines, and also had with him the newly introduced wax blank masters that replaced zinc discs.[22]

But his first experience, at a theatre in Calcutta, was underwhelming, and prompted him to record a sweeping generalisation in his diary: "I had yet to learn that the oriental ear was unappreciative of chords and harmonic treatment, and only demanded the rhythmic beat of the accompaniment of the drums. At this point we left."[23] At another point during his time in the city, he reflected somberly, and with the tone of someone who had arrived at a major revelation, that he had "entered a new world of musical and artistic values. One had to erase all memories of European opera houses: the very foundations of my musical training were undermined."[24] Fortuitously for him, he soon stumbled across the well-established vocalist Gauhar Jan, who sang in various languages and had mastered styles including *khayal*, *thumri*, *dadra* and *dhrupad*, and she rapidly became GTL's most prolifically marketed and popular artist.

These initial interactions between the GTL's representatives and the Indian musical community underscore how deeply the company was convinced of the commercial promise of recording, and the viability of seeking out musicians for its enterprise, despite a woefully thin knowledge of the nuances of the music itself. This is not to suggest that Indian musicians who did enter the recording business in the initial years were being necessarily exploited. Gauhar Jan, for instance, it is suspected, charged 1,000 rupees for a recording session, and Janakibai, a legendary musician from Allahabad, charged 3,000.[25] But Gaisberg's story indicates that a collision of jarringly different approaches to music was underway during the time when, as Gerry Farrell wryly phrases it, "The West thought India could be sold back to itself" through music.[26]

Revolutions Per Minute fast-forwards through this era, moving from the early Goan performers who set the stage for future ones to a time after recording was not a recent novelty. A second room housed discs about a woman whose legacy may not need an introduction: Kesarbai Kerkar, an early-twentieth century Goan musician who moved to Bombay at the age of 16 and became the most highly paid musician of her time. Although she was part of the *devadasi* tradition, she later learned from several gurus, including Alladiya Khan from the Jaipur-Atrauli *gharana*, and her style evolved over decades of training. That she continues to be one of most acclaimed figures in Hindustani music (her recording of a *hori*, "Jaat Kahan Ho," was chosen to

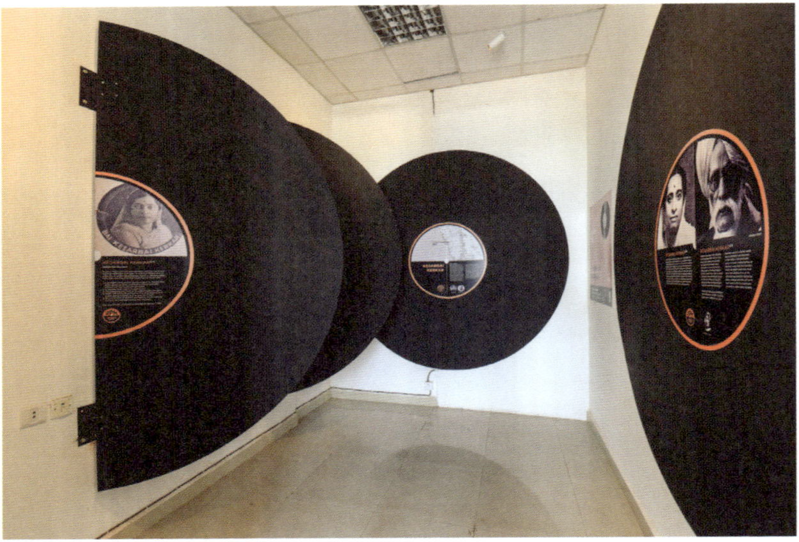

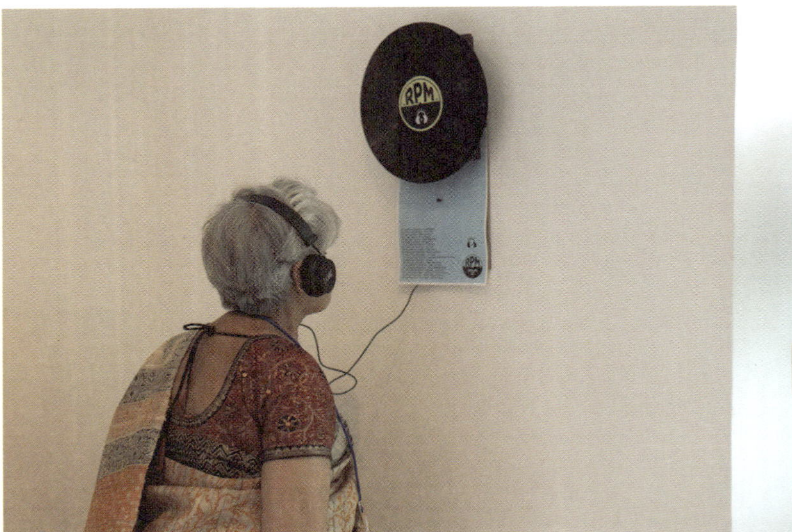
RPM

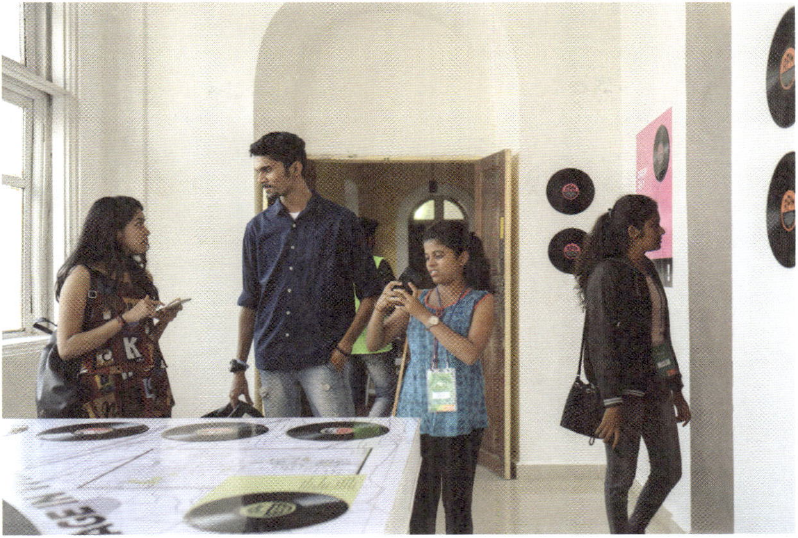

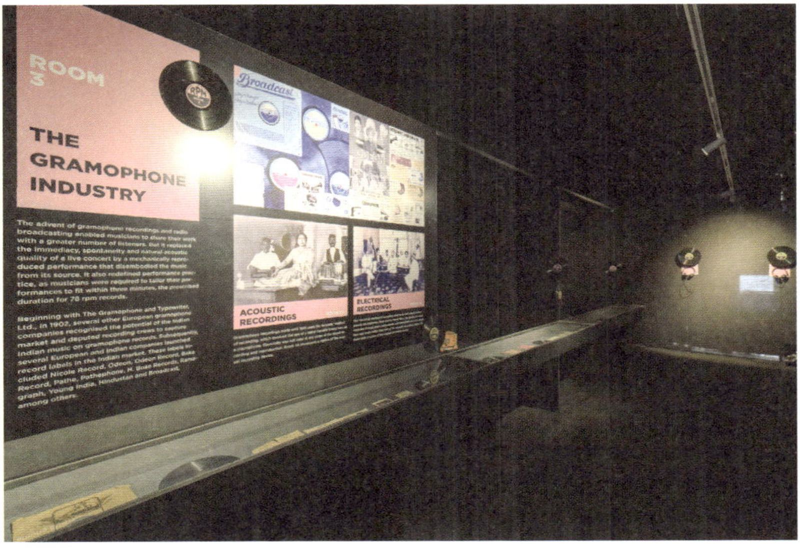
ROOM 3
THE GRAMOPHONE INDUSTRY
The advent of gramophone recordings and radio broadcasting enabled musicians to share their work with a greater number of listeners. But it replaced the immediacy, spontaneity and natural acoustic quality of a live concert by a mechanically reproduced performance that disembodied the music from its source. It also redefined performance practice, as musicians were required to tailor their performances to fit within three minutes, the prescribed duration for 78 rpm records.
Beginning with The Gramophone and Typewriter, Ltd., in 1902, several other European gramophone companies recognised the potential of the Indian market and deputed recording crews to capture Indian music on gramophone records. Subsequently, several European and Indian companies launched record labels in the Indian market. These labels included Nicole Record, Odeon, Odeon Record, Beka Record, Pathe, Pathephone, H. Bose Records, Ramagraph, Young India, Hindustan and Broadcast, among others.
Broadcast
ACOUSTIC RECORDINGS
ELECTRICAL RECORDINGS

represent Indian music on NASA's Voyager 1 spacecraft in 1977) was evident from the fact that an entire room of the exhibition had been devoted to her, containing details about her interrupted periods of training and brutally long practice regimens, and explaining why she is considered critical to the growth of Hindustani music.

Six of Kesarbai's tracks were available to listen to at the exhibition, through a headset. While listening to the last of these, "*Kaahe ko daari*," a *thumri* in *raag bhairavi*—the immensely popular morning raag that traditionally concluded performances—the haunting versatility of her voice stood out against the faint crackling of the recording. Because I had read in Namita Devidayal's *The Music Room* that Kesarbai felt antagonistic towards the way recording companies had preserved her work, and even deliberately muffled words to ensure that nobody used her recordings to copy her, there was also a surreal quality to the idea of listening to the recordings in such a distant space and context from those in which they were produced. Devidayal describes how Kesarbai was once infuriated that a shellac record of hers, initially made with HMV, was selling for a quarter of its price because the company had sold its stock to another label that dissolved and got rid of its excess stock. Though this can hardly be described as a brush with piracy, it made her resistant to the idea of recording until she was pleaded with years later by HMV.

This part of the exhibition also showcases an aspect of Pradhan's collaborative work on recovering music of this period. Kesarbai recorded tracks in the 1930s for a label called Broadcast. "We collaborated with the Society of Indian Record Collectors and digitised her earliest recordings," he told me. "Up until then, other than record collectors, most people had only heard her HMV recordings. But this was an important period in her life—immediately after she had learned from Alladiya Khan, and it shows how she made the transition in her style during that decade. By the time of the HMV recordings, her voice had also changed."

There are debates to be had about shifts in musical style that ensued after the arrival of the gramophone—for instance, scholars have wondered whether the music that was recorded on these discs are to be viewed as creations for the recording industry rather than accurate representations of performance tradition at the time.[27] For instance, the performance form shifted to adapt itself to the three-minute slots of time on RPM records, with the likely result that musicians attempted to demonstrate the most important aspects of their style. The longer sections of performances, such as the *aalaap* and *gat*, were sometimes made on separate recordings, and open-ended improvisation had to be cut back on.[28] With *Revolutions Per Minute*, Aneesh Pradhan and his collaborators aimed to lay out the crucial markers in the history of Hindustani classical music's transition to the era of recording, and how musicians grappled with these changes—a task that Pradhan mentioned is critical because he did not want to end up with "a hagiography of musicians from the past."

The final room of *Revolutions Per Minute* was modelled upon contemporary music-recording studios. One of the walls, which were painted black and had discs attached to them, had a summary of the unfolding of the gramophone industry. Pushkar Thakur, who worked with Pradhan to conceptualise its design, told me that the room was intended "as a celebration of the industry itself" and attempted to immerse the audience in the experience of recording music, while making it contemporary and relatable for the diverse age groups of people he envisioned as its audience.

The room was divided into two, with one half dedicated to the era—from the gramophone's introduction in India up to 1925—of acoustic recording, during which a metal horn was deployed instead of a microphone. The second part of the room displayed a replica of an electrical recording device, the more recent form of the gramophone that was developed during the First World War and used carbon-granule microphones. The most evocative construction of the room, though, was a series of long tables against the wall that showcased record covers and ads from companies that had forayed into Indian recording in the early-twentieth century. These included the British company Columbia and the German company Odeon, both of which arrived and attempted to establish labels in the Indian market in 1932, and featured advertisements of their recordings of Marathi music.[29] The record covers have images of the performers or drawings of well-dressed women with demure expressions, and reveal the sustained efforts by companies to make music look respectable and emphasise the status symbol of the gramophone. One of the images featured is a cover with GTL's iconic trademark of a dog listening to the gramophone called "His Master's Voice." Though these efforts may seem juvenile today, the company evidently mastered the technique of using illustrations in its catalogues to signify the aspirational quality of the gramophone. Somewhat bizarrely, it used a motley mix of imagery of middle-class homes, the goddesses Durga and Saraswati, and even one of the courts of Jahangir—in the ads, these figures are placed alongside an incongruous-looking gramophone. The seemingly impenetrable GTL met its match in Dharmatala in Calcutta, where, according to one account, a firm pirated an image of the HMV dog, though "with a slightly rabid look about him" and used it to sell gramophones.[30]

The exhibition focussed heavily on the commercial side of the industry to demonstrate, as Pradhan explained, that after the gramophone became a staple of the music industry, there was a dizzying amount of competition, collusion and rivalry between companies. GTL, for instance, released the same material under different labels, and there were court cases where artists were sued for having recorded the same material with more than one record label. "All recordings were owned by the companies. And you never know whether contracts said that the repertoire was owned by the companies too. There were even artists who signed off *raag yaman*—it didn't belong to them!" Pradhan said with a laugh.

The introduction of the gramophone sparked many other momentous developments besides this frenzied effort to monetise music. Listening was, according to the singer and author Vidya Shah, "democratised," as musicians could now share their work with larger audiences[31]; the stigma of being associated with the music profession may have lessened for women, as performances previously seen as degenerate became more mainstream[32]; listening to and learning from musicians became more plausible[33]; the advances in musical technology paved the way for the takeover of music by the film industry, and the introduction of amplifiers meant that the number of music festivals increased exponentially.

Anxieties about the future of Hindustani music, though, continued to appear. Pradhan details in his book that the music critic Vamanrao Deshpande, sounding eerily like our friend Sousa, mourned the moment that Hindustani music met with technology: "The record-player, radio, cinema and the loud-speaker, have now reached the common man. Its obvious consequence was the disappearance, at one stroke, of the harmony and the rapport between the audience and the singer.... This process of technology has only contributed to the lowering of the quality of music."[34]

An element that Deshpande appears to have overlooked here in his concern about the loss—of authenticity and the rapport of performance—is that, in a way, the introduction of the gramophone was followed by a revamped performance tradition. The formation of music circles in the early-twentieth century altered forms of patronage considerably. Concerts moved from homes to public spaces, and by the 1940s, were entrenched in Bombay's musical culture. But, as the scholar Dard Neuman points out, several twentieth-century musicians cite recordings of artists they heard on the gramophone, or through the radio, as their early inspirations. And one instance, where Murad Khan demanded to hear his recording during a live broadcast, indicates that it is difficult to divorce this later concert culture from the impact the gramophone had already had on ways of listening.[35]

Notes

[1] John Philip Sousa, "The Menace of Mechanical Music," *Appleton's Magazine* 8 (1906): 278.

[2] Dard Neuman, "The Production of Aura in the Gramophone Age of the 'Live' Performance," *Asian Music* 40, no. 2 (2009): 119.

[3] Namita Devidayal, *The Music Room* (Random House India, 2007).

[4] T. G. Percival Spear, "The Mutiny and Great Revolt of 1857-59," *Encyclopaedia Britannica*, https://www.britannica.com/place/India/The-mutiny-and-great-revolt-of-1857-59; See also: William Wilson Hunter, *The Indian Empire: Its People, History, and Products* (New Delhi: Asian Educational Services, 2005).

[5] Aneesh Pradhan, *Hindustani Music in Colonial Bombay* (Three Essays Collective, 2014), 4-9.

[6] Pradhan, *Hindustani Music in Colonial Bombay.*

[7] Tejaswini Niranjana, "Musicophilia and the Lingua Musica in Mumbai," *Cultural Studies* 32, no. 2 (2018): 6.

[8] Sebastian Klotz, Philip V Bohlman, Lars-Christian Koch (eds.), *Sounding Cities: Auditory Transformations in Berlin, Chicago and Kolkata* (Zurich: Lit Verlag, 2018), 181.

[9] Sumana Ramanan, "A Tale of Two Cultures," *The Caravan*, April 01, 2015, https://caravanmagazine.in/reviews-essays/tale-two-cultures-hindustani-music.

[10] Pradhan, *Hindustani Music in Colonial Bombay*, 24.

[11] Pradhan, *Hindustani Music in Colonial Bombay*, 19.

[12] Pradhan, *Hindustani Music in Colonial Bombay*, 36.

[13] Pradhan, *Hindustani Music in Colonial Bombay*, 33.

[14] Pradhan, *Hindustani Music in Colonial Bombay*, 41.

[15] Pradhan, *Hindustani Music in Colonial Bombay*, 39.

[16] Daniel M Neuman, *The Life of Music in North India: The Organization of an Artistic Tradition* (Chicago: The University of Chicago Press, 1990), 216.

[17] Pradhan, *Hindustani Music in Colonial Bombay*, 39.

[18] Gerry Farrell, *Indian Music and the West* (Oxford: Oxford University Press: 1997), 114.

[19] Michael S Kinnear, *The Gramophone Company's First Indian Recordings 1899 – 1908* (Bombay: Popular Prakashan, 1994), 29.

[20] Farrell, *Indian Music and the West*, 116.

[21] GN Joshi, "A Concise History of the Phonograph Industry in India," *Popular Music* 7, no. 2 (1997) : 149.

[22] In his essay "A Concise History of the Phonograph Industry in India," GN Joshi explains the mechanics of this process: "In the initial stages gramophone recording was done by a process of "zinc etching." A zinc disc with a smooth and shiny surface was coated with a layer of fat on which spiral grooves were cut by a stylus. The stylus was fixed to a diaphragm that vibrated in sympathy with sound waves of the song and music, sung or played into the large mouth of a horn. The recorded zinc disc was then immersed in acid for about ten minutes and the spiral grooves of music were etched on the surface. This disc record could then be played back straight away." Joshi, "A Concise History of the Phonograph Industry in India," 147.

[23] Farrell, *Indian Music and the West*, 116.

[24] Farrell, *Indian Music and the West*, 116.

[25] Farrell, *Indian Music and the West*, 119.

[26] Farrell, *Indian Music and the West*, 112.

[27] Farrell, *Indian Music and the West*, 142.

[28] Pradhan, *Hindustani Music in Colonial Bombay*, 187; Gerry Farrell, *Indian Music and the West*, 136.

[29] Joshi, "A Concise History of the Phonograph Industry in India," 150.

[30] Farrell, *Indian Music and the West*, 146.

[31] Swati Daftuar, "Catalysts of Change," *The Hindu*, last updated October 18, 2016, https://www.thehindu.com/features/friday-review/Catalysts-of-change/article14425996.ece.

[32] Farrell, *Indian Music and the West*, 124.

[33] Vidya Shah, *Jalsa: Indian Women and their Journeys from the Salon to the Studio* (New Delhi: Tulika Books, 2016).

[34] Pradhan, *Hindustani Music in Colonial Bombay*, 207.

[35] Neuman, "The Production of Aura in the Gramophone Age of the 'Live' Performance," *Asian Music* 40, no. 2 (2009) : 110.

Biographies

Akhila Vimal C. is a PhD candidate at Jawaharlal Nehru University, New Delhi. Her research interests are disfiguration and staging of relationalities of disability, gender, and caste in textual and performance practices of India. Her articles have been published in various journals, such as the essay "Prosthetic Rasa: Dance on Wheels and Challenged Kinesthetics" in *Research in Drama Education* (*RiDE*), and "Performing Disfiguration: Construction of The 'Primitive' And The Ambiguities Of Representing Pain In Kathakali" in *Journal of Emerging Dance Scholarship* (*JEDS*).

Amitava Sanyal is recovering from journalism after 20 years of constant writing and editing. He has written on arts for various publications, including a music column for Hindustan Times for a few years. He has been a Chevening journalism scholar and a New India Foundation fellow.

Maya Palit is a Delhi-based journalist who shuttles between writing and editing. She has worked in non-fiction publishing houses and digital newsrooms and is presently Books Editor at The Caravan magazine. Among her interests are fiction-writing, poetry and music. She studied literature—specialising in South African and Caribbean literature, blues music and science fiction—and might return to it someday.

About Projects/Processes

Projects/Processes is an initiative launched by Serendipity Arts Foundation in 2017 to publish commissioned research essays, longform writing, and in-depth criticism that explore the ideas and processes behind select curatorial projects at Serendipity Arts Festival. Over three years, the Festival has accumulated a rich database of creative energies and partnerships. As an eight-day long event, the Festival is a platform for multidisciplinary collaboration and cultural innovation, and has commissioned over 90 new works across the visual and performing arts since its inception in 2016. The Projects/Processes series offers an opportunity to give some of these works and the stories that they tell continued life, through a deeply engaged look at how they came together and their significance to the discourse of contemporary art in India moving forward. Each volume comprises essays covering distinct projects that stand in some dialogue with each other, through the questions they raise and the thematic landscape they cover.

Project Head & Editor: Senjuti Mukherjee
Managing Editor: Nandita Jaishankar
Copy editors: Arnav Adhikari & Arushi Vats
Cover design and layout: Aman Srivastava

Projects/Processes as an initiative is conceptualised and supported by Mr. S. K. Munjal, Founder Patron, Serendipity Arts Foundation and Ms. Smriti Rajgarhia, Director, Serendipity Arts Foundation.

About Serendipity Arts Festival

Serendipity Arts Festival (SAF) is one of the largest multi-disciplinary arts initiatives in the South Asian region. It spans the visual, performing and culinary arts, whilst exploring genres with film, live arts, literature and fashion. Besides the core content, which is conceptualised by an eminent curatorial panel, the Festival has various layers of programming, in the form of educational initiatives, workshops, special projects, and institutional engagements. Through active conversations between the artistic community and the urban, social landscape, the festival continues to evolve around the mandate of making art visible and accessible. The festival seeks collaborations at its core, inspiring new perspectives of seeing and experiencing. The Festival is a cultural experiment that also addresses issues such as arts education, patronage culture, interdisciplinary discourse, inclusivity and accessibility of the arts.

About Serendipity Arts Foundation

Serendipity Arts Foundation is an organisation that facilitates pluralistic cultural expressions, sparking conversations around the arts across the South Asian region. Committed to innovation and creativity, the aim of the Foundation is to support practice and research in the arts, as well as to promote sustainability and education in the field through a range of cultural and collaborative initiatives. The Foundation hosts projects through the year, which include institutional partnerships with artists and art organisations, educational initiatives, grants and outreach programmes across India.